AF552550

INDIA BOOKVARSITY
LOTUS CHOICES
Editor: Mahendra Kulasrestha

The VITAL TRUTHS of Hinduism

Sister Nivedita

A Note By
MAHATMA GANDHI

Introductrion by
Rabindranath Tagore

'... almost the only fair account of Hindu society written in English.'

—Ananda K.Coomaraswamy

Swami Vivekananda's star performer Sister Nivedita's masterly analysis presented in the correct focus and instead of an haphazard collection, to bring forward and underline her unusually different and significant contribution to the understanding of Hindu religion, culture and way of life not done till date.

4735/22, Prakash Deep Building
Ansari Road, Darya Ganj,
New Delhi-110002

THE VITAL TRUTHS of Hinduism

SISTER NIVEDITA

Source: ***The Web of Indian Life*** **and** ***Footfalls of Indian History***
By Sister Nivedita, 1915, Advaita Ashrama, Mayawati, Almora, Himalayas

The Vital Truths of Hinduism,
by Sister Nivedita

First Edition—2011
ISBN: 978-81-8382-271-8 (H/B)

Lotus Press Publishers & Distributors
Unit No. 220, Second Floor, 4735/22,
Prakash Deep Building, Ansari Road,
Darya Ganj, New Delhi-10002
Ph.: 011-23280047, 32903912 • Mob.: 098118-38000
E-mail: lotus_press@sify.com

Laser Typeset by: **Upasana Graphics**, Delhi
Printed at: **Concept Inprint**, Delhi

Gandhi Meets Nivedita

Because he became 'Mahatma' in later years, Gandhi's reference to meeting Sister Nivedita—in 1901, when he was 31 and visiting Calcutta to attend the Congress session—acquires a special interest, and though trivial, it is noted here:

"... it was impossible to be satisfied without seeing Swami Vivekananda. So with great enthusiasm I went to Belur Math, mostly...on foot. I loved the sequestered site of the Math. I was disappointed and sorry to be told that the Swami was at his Calcutta house, lying ill, and could not be seen.

"I then ascertained the place of residence of Sister Nivedita, and met her in a Chowrighee mansion. *I was taken aback at the splendour that surrounded her,* and even in our conversation, there was not much meeting ground,... I met her again at Mr. Pestonji Padshah's place. I happened to come in just as she was talking to his old mother, and so I became an interpreter between the two. In spite of my failure to find any agreement with her, I could not but notice and admire her overflowing love for Hinduism. I came to know of her books later."

EDITORSPEAK

Not Sufficiently Recognised

Human life remains a mystery, and will remain so till one doesn't know when. The material the human being is made of, is the same everywhere, but has been kneaded differently in every community by a variety of open and hidden factors and given different shapes, which we name as 'cultures'; though the fact that all cultures are different, has yet to be recognised by History. The Hindu, Buddhist, Christian, Islamic and others are all different in their basic understanding of religion coming out of it to sustain it, the values emerging from these, the life styles organised around these—some toterant and non-violent, others killing others as well as themselves—like the Inca, Aztec, Maya, etc., of South American lands (who killed their young every morning so that the sun would rise—and thousands on special occasions) some fanatically anti-idol, some deriding all others to the extent of massacring their followers totally, etc.

The earlier century has been the century of religious studies, in which Hinduism has played a critical role courtesy chiefly of Swami Vivekananda, whose appearance at the Parliament of Religions in 1893 in Chicago, created a veritable movement in favour of Vedanta and a possible world religion based on it. His several western female disciples, Margaret E. Noble, or Sister Nivedita, among them, made their mark by devoting their lives to the cause of religion as well as the advancement of people related to it.

Nivedita, a school-teacher in England, came to India in 1898, and stayed here till her death in 1911, standing on her own after the Master's rather early demise in 1902. She started a girls' school and took interest in the Indian situation. The freedom movement was slowly rising, and though she did not herself take active part in it, she did a lot to inspire people by delivering lectures in several cities, including Calcutta. Her residence and school became a centre of such activities; she came to know all significant political leaders of the time. She thus in a way compensated her Master's agenda which was woefully lacking in this area; it is surprising that the Swami did not recognise the need of independence from the foreign yoke; Tagore also did not do enough in this area—a point which is conveniently ignored. But the foreign nun was fast in recognising this lacuna and tried her best to fill it up in ample measure.

The vital truths of Hindu religion and culture —'The most perfect thought the world ever produced'—as analysed, understood and dileneated by Sister Nivedita, the star performer of the pioneer scholar-warrior saint Vivekanada of the 1893 Chicago Parliament of Religions fame, presents them in the following pages in a most striking and eye-opening manner unsurpassed by any till now after a century of her passing away. The originality of her observations, as in the case of the much derided caste system, the Hindu woman, the Trimurti systhesis, Buddhism and the Shiva concept, are mind-shaking in their essentials—and her view that the caste system should be revived in a modified form, to 'regain India's lost national efficiency.'

It is worth underlinning that the great man of Indian Renaissance, Tagore, had also commended the caste, though on a different ground, and we in the present times, must give it a serious revisionary thought. The Sister's summary of the caste discussion can form the basic of such further work and planning. She concludes: "'''' great benefits as well as great evils have accrued from caste. It is an institution that **makes the Hindu society the most eclectic with regards to ideas in the world. In India all religions have taken refuge**—the Parsis before the tide of Mussalman conquest, the Christians of Syria; the Jews. **And they have received more that shelter**—they have had the hospitality of a world that had nothing to fear from the foreigner who came in the name of freedom of conscience. Caste made this possible, for in one sense it is the social formulation of defence minus all agreements of aggression. **Caste is race-continuity; it is the historic sense; it is the dignity of tradition** and of purpose for the future. It is even more; it is the familiarity of a whole people in all its grades with the one supreme human motive—the notion of *noblesse oblige.*' (Emphasis mine)

It may be added that nowhere else has been any such experiment in deliberate social organisation, which, it would seem, has been a great lacuna—as every human born came to be automatically regarded as divine, having all the rights—but notduly or even good behaviour requirement towards others. Which in history resulted in a character of violence, attack on others and wars. India did not develop a culture of war; she never attacked any other community or nation, a drawback resulting in great oppression and suffering. And now, the horrifying demon of Terrorism stalking the whole world.

Some kind of human organisation and management would seem a basic need of society and people at large, and caste was an experiment in the line.

Her's was a genuine case of deep enchantment with a foreign culture, including the arts. Her visit to Ajanta convinced her of the intrinsic merit of Hindu culture; her long article on Ajanta very ably presented the case of Indian art for future generations. She got actively involved in the Indian art movement by inspiring Abanindranath Tagore, Nandlal Bose and their ilk to study and inculcate the beauty of Ajanta in the new art movement developing at that time. This is another aspect of her life which should be duly underlined and given its due.

She was basically a scholar and studied Hindu religion and society with due deligence, and published these in half a dozen quality books. Being a foreigner's view, these writings present the material in a more forthright and clear-cut manner than the work of others, and the present writer is of the view that her writings should be properly edited and republished, with relevant notings. One such attempt, a minor one, is the present selection of articles under a different planning. The matters of culture are critical, and all cultures being fundamentally as well as physically different, their basics and follow-ups should be carefully sorted out and put to comparative examination. Hindu culture is fast being recognised as a culture of accomodation, and some are looking at it as 'a future United Nations' to informally settle differences.

It was striking to find in the well known American magazine 'Newsweek' early this year the detailing of a dispute in that country as that America was being Hinduised. Perhaps a significant reward to our culture in modern times!

So understand Hinduism in its basic philosophy and social structure, underline its strong points, rejecting the harmful ones, redoing it according to modern needs, giving it further universal dimensions, and promoting it worldwide like Vivekananda tried to do but could not owing chiefly to health reasons, which took its toll early in his life (and the gods—the goddess in particular whom he worshipped—did not help him) the mission may be revived. Amen!

Hindu Culture

Caste system is good
and should be revised
with modifications

•

The Hindu woman was an
Ideal embodiment of female
social reponsibility and behaviour

•

Marriage is like entering the
church for women

•

The fear of female curse
Is widespread

•

India is always a systhesis

•

Goddess Shitala rides a donkey,
and the animal has words in the
Indian languages, because there were
no horses in that dim past

•

The Shiva cult is the Hinduisation of the
Budda image.

•

Kanheri was a university and Elephanta was a
Cathedral, both appenages of some royal seat.

The Great- hearted Western Woman

Rabindranath Tagore

Indians, like all other peoples of the world, are naturally susceptible to flattery. But, unfortunately, they have been deprived of their share of it, even in wholesome measure, both by the Fates presiding at the making of their history as well as by the guests partaking of their salt. We have been declared inefficient in practical matters by our governors, foreign missionaries have created a vast literature proclaiming our moral obliquity, while casual visitors have expressed their opinion that we are particularly uninteresting to the intellectual mind of the West.

Other peoples' estimate of our work is a great part of our world, and the most important other peoples in the present age being the Europeans, it has become tragic in its effect for us to be unable to evoke their appreciation. There was a time when India could touch the most sensitive part of Europe's mind by storming her imagination with a gorgeous vision of wealth. But cruel time has done its work and the golden illusion has vanished, leaving the ragged poverty of India open to public inspection, charitable or otherwise. Therefore, epithets of a disparaging nature from the West find an easy target in India, bespattering her skin and piercing her vital parts.

Epithets once given circulation die hard, for they have their breeding-places in our mental laziness and in our natural readiness to believe that whatever is different from ourselves must be offensive. Men can live through and die happy in spite of disparagement, if it comes from critics with whom they have no dealings.

But unfortunately our critics not only have the power to give us a bad name, but also to hang us. They play the part of Providence over three hundred millions of aliens whose language they hardly know, and with whom their acquaintance is of the surface. Therefore, the vast accumulation of calumny against India, continually growing and spreading over the earth, secretly and surely obstructs the element of heart from finding an entrance into our government.

One can never do justice from a mere sense of duty, to those for whom one lacks respect. And human beings, as we are, justice is not the chief thing that we claim from our rulers. We need sympathy as well, in order to feel that we have human relationship with them thus retain as much of our self-respect as may be possible.

For some time past a spirit of retaliation has taken possession of our literature and our social world. We have furiously begun to judge our judges, and the judgement comes from hearts sorely stricken with hopeless humiliation. And because our thoughts have an organ whose sound does not reach outside our country, or even the ears of our governors within its boundaries, their expression is growing in vehemence. The prejudice cultivated on the side of the powerful is no doubt dangerous for the weak, but it cannot be wise on the part of the strong to ignore that thorny crop grown on the opposite field. The upsetting of truth in the relationship of the ruler and the ruled can never be compensated by the power that lies in the grip of the mailed fist.

And this was the reason which made us deeply grateful of Sister Nivedita, that great-hearted Western woman, when she gave utterance to her criticism of Indian life. She had won her access to the inmost heart of our society by her supreme gift of sympathy. She did not come to us with the impertinent curiosity of a visitor, nor did she elevate herself on a special high perch with the idea that a bird's eye view is truer than the human view because of its superior aloofness. She lived our life and came to know us by becoming one of ourselves. She became so intimately familiar with our people that she had the rare opportunity of observing us unawares. As a race we have our special limitations and imperfections, and for a foreigner it does not require a high degree of keen-sightedness to detect them. We know for certain that these defects did not escape Nivedita's observation, but she did not stop there to generalise, as most other foreigners do. And because she had a comprehensive mind and extraordinary insight of love she could see the creative ideals at work behind our social forms and discover our soul that has living connection with its past and is marching towards its fulfilment.

But Sister Nivedita, being an idealist, saw a great deal more than is usually seen by those foreigners who can only see things, but not truths. Therefore, I have heard her being discredited by the authority of long experience, which is merely an experience of blindness carried through long years. And of these I have the same words to say which I said to those foreign residents of Japan, whose long experience itself was like a film obscuring the freshness of their sight, making them conscious of only some outer details, specially where they irritated their minds. Instead of looking on the picture side of the canvas, if they look on the blank side, it will not give any more value to their view because of the prolonged period of their staring.

The mental sense, by the help of which we feel the spirit of a people, is like the sense of sight, or of touch—it is a natural gift. It finds its objects, not by analysis, but by direct apprehension. Those who have this vision merely see events and facts, and not their inner association. Those who have no ear when, by reason of the mere lengthiness of their suffering, they threaten to establish the fact of the tune to be a noise, one need not be anxious about the reputation of a longer time to develop their tangles, while the right answer comes promptly.

It is a truism to say that shadows accompany light. What you feel as the truth of a people, has its numberless contradictions, just as the single fact of the roundness of earth is contradicted by the innumerable arranged and heaped up into loads of contradiction; yet men having faith in the reality of ideals hold firmly that the vision of truth does not depend upon its dimension, but upon its vitality. And Sister Nivedita has uttered the vital truths about Indian life.

CONTENTS

Sister Nivedita popularised
The art of India

1

MY ENTRANCE INTO HINDU LIFE

A house of my own, in which to eat, sleep, and conduct a girls' school, and full welcome accorded at any hour of day or night that I might choose to invade the privacy of a group of women friends: these were the conditions under which I made my entrance into Hindu life in the city of Calcutta. I came when the great autumn feast of the Mother was past; I was there at the ending of the winter when plague broke out in our midst, and the streets at night were thronged with seething multitudes, who sang strange litanies and went half mad with religious excitement; I remained through the terrific heat, when activity became a burden, and only one's Hindu friends understood how to live; I left my home for a time when the tropical rains had begun, and in the adjoining roads the cab-horses were up to their girths in water hour after hour.

What a beautiful old world it was in which I spent those months! It moved slowly, to a different rhythm from anything that one had known. It was a world in which a great thought or intense emotion was held as the true achievement, distinguishing the day as no deed could. It was a world in which men in loincloths, seated on door-sills in dusty lanes, said things about

Shakespeare and Shelley that some of us would go far to hear. It was full of gravity, simplicity, and the solid and enduring reality of great character and will.

From all round the neighbourhood at sunset would come the sound of gongs and bells in the family-chapel of each house, announcing Evensong. At that same hour might the carpenter be seen censing his tools, or the schoolboy, perhaps, his inkstand and pen, as if thanking these humble creatures of the day's service; and women on their way to worship would stop wherever a glimpse of the Ganges was possible, or before a bo-tree or tulsi-plant, to salute it, joining their hands and bowing the head. More and more, **as the spirit of Hindu culture became the music of life, did this hour and that of sunrise grow to be the events of my day.** One learns in India to believe in what Maeterlinck calls "the great active silence", and in such moments consciousness, descending like a plummet into the deeps of personality, and leaving even thought behind, seems to come upon the unmeasured and immeasurable.

The centre of gravity is shifted. The scene reveals itself as what India declares it, merely the wreckage of the Unseen, cast up on the shores of Time and Space. Nothing that happens within the activity of daylight can offer a counter-attraction to this experience. But then, as we must not forget, the Indian day is pitched in its key. Tasks are few, and are to be performed with dignity and earnestness. Everything has its aureole of associations. **Eating and bathing —with us chiefly selfish operations—are here great sacramental acts,** guarded at all points by social honour and the passion of purity. From sunrise to sunset the life of the nation moves on, and the hum of labour and the clink of tools rise up, as in some vast monastery, accompanied by the chanting of prayers and the atmosphere of recollectedness.

The change itself from daylight to darkness is incredibly swift. A few fleecy clouds gather on the horizon and pass from white, may be, to orange and even crimson. Then the sun descends, and at once we are alone with the deep purple, the tremulous stars of the Indian night. Far away in the North, hour after hour, outlines go on cutting themselves clearer against the green and opal sky, and long low cliffs grow slowly dim with shadows on the sea. The North has Evening: the South, Night.

Tropical thunderstorms are common through April and May at the day's end, and the terrible convulsion of Nature that then rages for an hour or two gives a simple parallel to many instances of violent contrast and the logical extreme in Indian art and history. This is a land where men will naturally spend the utmost that is in them. And yet side by side with the scarlet and gold of the loom, how inimitably delicate is the blending of tints in the tapestry! It is so with Indian life. The most delicate nuance and remorseless heroism exist side by side, and are equally recognised and welcomed.

The foundation-stone of our knowledge of a people must be an understanding of their region. For social structure depends primarily on labour, and labour is necessarily determined by place. Thus we reach the secret of thought and ideals. As an example of this we have only to see how the Northman, with his eyes upon the sun, carries into Christianity the great cycle of fixed feasts that belongs to Midsummer's Day and Yule, approximately steady in the solar year; while the child of the South, to whom the lunar sequence is everything, contributes Easter and Whitsuntide. The same distinction holds in the history of Science, where savants are agreed that in early astronomy the sun elements were first worked out in Chaldea and the moon in India.

The woman pausing in the dying light to salute the river brings us to another such instance. There is nothing occult in the passion of Hindus for the Ganges. Sheer delight in physical coolness, the joy of the eyes, and the gratitude of the husbandman made independent of rain, are sufficient basis. But when we add to this the power of personification common to naive peoples, and the peculiarly Hindu genius of idealism, the whole gamut of associations is accounted for. Indeed, it would be difficult to live long beside the Ganges and not fall under the spell of her personality. Yellow, leonine, imperious, there is in her something of the caprice, of the almost treachery, of beautiful women who have swayed the wills of the world. Semiramis, Cleopatra, Mary Stuart, are far from being the Hindu ideal, but the power of them all is in that great mother whom India worships. For to the simple, the Ganges is completely mother. Does she not give life and food? To the pious she is the bestower of purity, and as each bather steps into her flood, he stoops tenderly to place a little of the water on his head, craving pardon with words of salutation for the touch of his foot.

To the philosopher she is the current of his single life, sweeping irresistibly onward to the universal. To the travelled she tells of Banaras and the mountain snows, and legends of Shiva the Great God, and Uma Haimavati, mother of all womanhood. Or she brings memories of the Indian Christ and His youth among the shepherds in the forests of Vrindaban on her tributary Jamuna. And to the student of history she is the continuity of Aryan thought and civilisation through the ages, giving unity and meaning to the lives of races and centuries as she passes through them, carrying the message of the past ever into the future, a word of immense promise, an assurance of unassailable certainty.

But with all this and beyond it all, the Ganges, to her lovers, is a person. To us, who have fallen so far away from the Greek mode of seeing, this is difficult perhaps to understand. But living in a Calcutta lane the powers of the imagination revive; the moon-setting becomes again. Selene riding on the horse with the veiled feet; Phrebus Apollo rising out of one angle of a pediment is a convincing picture of the morning sky; and the day comes when one surprises oneself in the act of talking with earth and water as conscious living beings. One is ready now to understand the Hindu expression of love for river and home. It is a love with which the day's life throbs.

"Without praying, no eating! Without bathing, no praying!" is the short strict rule to which every woman at least conforms; hence the morning bath in the river is the first great event of the day. It is still dark when little companies of women of rank begin to leave their houses on foot for the bathing stairs. These are the proud and high-bred on whom "the sun has never looked". Too sensitive to tolerate the glance of passers by, and too faithful to forego the sanctifying immersion, they cut the knot of both difficulties at once in this way. Every moment of the ablution has its own invocation, and the return journey is made, carrying a brass vessel full of the sacred water which will be used all day to sprinkle the place in which any one eats or prays.

Their arrival at home finds already waiting those baskets of fruit and flowers which are to be used in worship; for one of the chief acts of Hindu devotion consists in burying the feet of the adored in flowers. The feet, from their contact with all the dusty and painful ways of the world, have come to be lowliest and most despised of all parts of the body, while the head is so sacred that only a superior may touch it. To take the dust of the feet of the saints or of an image, therefore, and put it upon one's head, is emblematic of all reverence and sense of unworthiness, and eager love will often address itself to the "lotus-feet" of the beloved. Amongst my own friends, health forbade the bathing before dawn, and poverty did not allow of the visit to the river in closed *palkee* (palanquin) every day. But half-past nine or ten always found the younger women busy bringing incense and flowers and Ganges water for the mother's Puja, as it is called; and then, while she performed the daily ceremonies, they proceeded to make ready the fruits and sweets which were afterwards to be blessed and distributed.

It is interesting to see the difference between temple and a church. The former may seem absurdly small, for theoretically it is simply a covered shrine which contains one or other of certain images or symbols, before which appropriate offerings are made and prescribed rituals performed by duly appointed priests. The table is only properly called an altar in temples of the Mother; in other cases it would be more correct perhaps to speak of the throne, since fruit and flowers are the only sacrifices permitted. So it is clear that the Eastern temple corresponds to that part of the Christian church which is known technically as the sanctuary. The worshipper is merely incidental here; he sits or kneels on the steps, and pays the priest to perform for him some special office; or he reads and contemplates the image in a spirit of devotion. The church, on the other hand, includes shrine and congregation, and has more affinity to the Muslim mosque, which is simply a Church with the nave unroofed.

Temples are not very popular in Bengal, every house being supposed to have its chapel or oratory, for which the ladies care, unless the family be rich enough to maintain a chaplain. Even the services of a Brahmin in the house or neighbourhood, however, will not dispense them from the offering of elaborate personal puja before the morning meal can be thought of.

Just as the housewives of some European university town in the Middle Ages would feel responsible for the welfare of the "poor scholar", so to the whole of Hindu society, which has assimilated in its own way the functions of the university, the religious student is a common burden. Where he is, there is the university, and he must be supported by the nearest householders. For this reason, I, being regarded as a student of their religion, my good neighbours were unfailing of kindness in the matter of household supplies. Perhaps the most striking instance of this lay in the fact that when I was to have a guest I had only to say so, and friends in the vicinity would send in a meal ready-cooked, or the necessary bedding, without my even knowing the names of those to whom I owed the bounty. And with all this, there was no question as to the course of my study or the conclusions I was reaching—no criticism, either, of its form. They simply accorded to a European woman the care they were accustomed to bestow on the ashen-clad ascetic, because they understood that some kind of disinterested research was her object also, and they knew so well that the management of affairs was no part of the function of the scholar. What do we not read of the depth of a culture that is translated and reapplied with such ease as this? And what do we not learn of the intellectual freedom and development of the people?

Few things, even in Indian life, are so interesting as this matter of the social significance of the beggar. That distaste for property which we see in such lives as Kant's and Spinoza's resolves itself readily in the Indian climate into actual destitution. Shelter and clothing are hardly necessities there: a handful of rice and a few herbs such as can be obtained at any door are alone indispensable. But everything conspires to throw upon such as beg the duty of high thinking and the exchange of ideas with their supporters. Hence the beggar makes himself known by standing in the courtyard and singing some hymn or prayer. He comes always, that is to say, in the Name of God.

There is a whole literature of these beggars' songs, quaint and simple, full of what we in Europe call the Celtic spirit. In this lowest aspect, therefore, the Indian beggar is the conserver of the folk-poetry of his country. Where his individuality is strong, however, he is much more. To the woman who serves him he is then the religious teacher, talking with her of subjects on which she can rarely converse, and in this way carrying the highest culture far and wide.

It is droll to find that the whole city is parcelled out into wards, each of which is visited regularly on a given day. My days were Wednesday and Sunday, and going out one of these mornings about nine, I was fortunate enough to catch the whole procession coming up the lane. Men and women they were, elderly for the most part, but hale and well, with their long staffs in the right hand, and metal or wooden bowls in the left amongst the most cheerful human beings I ever saw. The fact of this regular division of the city puts the affair at once on the basis of a poor-rate (of which we have none in India), and shows that in ways appropriate to themselves the Hindu people are as able organisers as any.

It may be that in Western cities the work-house is a necessary solution, but certainly this Indian distribution of want over the wealthier community, with its joining of the act of giving to the natural sentiment, seems a good deal less mechanical and more humane than ours. It is very amusing sometimes to see how tenacious people are of their own superstitions.

I have seen an English woman made really unhappy because an Indian beggar would not accept a loaf she bought and handed to him, while he would have been very thankful for the money that it cost. The donor and her friends were in despair at what they regarded as utterly impracticable. Yet to the onlooker it seemed that the obstinacy was on their own side. In England we are warned that alcohol is a constant temptation to the poor and ill-fed; it is better, therefore, to give food than money. In India, on the other hand, there is no risk whatever on this score; for not one man in a hundred ever tasted liquor, and at the same time a Hindu beggar at least may not eat bread made with yeast, or baked by any but Hindus of his own or better caste. Now the offering made in this case was of yeast-made bread, baked by a Mohammedan, and handled by a Christian! To the poor man it was evident that the lady was willing to give; why should she load her gift with impossible conditions? And for my own part I could but echo, why?

Among the quaintest customs are those of the night-beggars. These are Mohammedans, but all fields are their pasture. They carry a bowl and a lamp as their insignia of office. It is common amongst these gentlemen to fix on a sum at sunset that they deem sufficient for their modest wants, and to vow that they shall know no rest till this is gathered.

Like a strong tide beating through the months, rise and fall the twelve or thirteen great religious festivals, or pujas. Chief of them all, in Bengal, is the autumn Durga-Puja, or Festival of the Cosmic Energy. A later month is devoted to the thought of all that is gentle and tender in the Motherhood of Nature. Again it is the Indian Minerva, Saraswati, who claims undivided attention. Those who have lived in Lancashire will remember how the aspect of streets and cottages is changed towards Simnel Sunday. Every window is decorated with cakes, and every cake bears a spirited picture in comfits of some coaching or other local scene. And everywhere, with us at Christmas-time, the shops are gay with holly and mistletoe, so that there is no mistaking the time of year. Similarly, in Calcutta, as each puja comes round, characteristic articles appear in the bazaars. At one time it is hand-screens made of beetles' wings and peacocks' feathers and every shop and every pedlar seems to carry these beautiful fans. Through September and October, as the Durga-Puja approaches, the streets resound with carols to the Mother. But the most charming of all is the Farewell Procession with the Image.

For no image may be kept more than the prescribed number of days, usually three. Up to the evening before the feast it is not sacred at all, and anyone may touch it. Then, however, a Brahmin, who has fasted all day, meditates before the figure, and, as it is said, "magnetises" it. The texts he chalets are claimed to be aids to the concentration of his own mind, and to have no other function. When the image has been consecrated it becomes a sacred object, but even then it is not actually worshipped. Its position is that of a stained-glass window, or an altar-piece, in an Anglican church. It is a suggestion offered to devout thought and feeling. On the step before it stands a brass pitcher full of water, and the mental effort of the worshipper is directed upon this water; for even so, it is said, does the formless Divine fill the Universe.

It would seem that the Hindu mind is very conscious of the possibility that the image may thwart its own intention and become an idol; for not only is this precaution taken in the act of adoration, but it is directed that at the end of the Puja it shall be conveyed away and thrown bodily into the river! On the third evening, therefore, towards sunset, the procession forms itself, little contingents joining it from every house in the village as it passes the door, each headed by one or two men bearing the figure of the god or goddess, and followed by the children of the family and others. It is a long winding march to the Ganges' side. Arrived there, the crown is carefully removed, to be kept a year for good luck; and then, stepping down into the stream, the bearers heave up their load and throw it as far as they can. We watch the black hair bobbing up and down in the current for a while, and then, often amid the tears of the children, turn back to the house from which a radiant guest has departed. There is quietness now where for three days have been worship and feasting. But the tired women are glad to rest from the constant cooking, and even the babies are quickly cheered, for it will be but a month or two till some new festival shall bring to them fresh stores of memory.

The great decorum of Oriental life is evident when one has to come or go through a Hindu city in the evening. Doorways and windows are ranked with broad stone benches, and here, after the evening meal, sit umbers of men in earnest conversation. But any woman is safe in such a street. Not even the freedom of a word or look will be offered. As Lakshman, in the great Epic, recognised among the jewels of Sita only her anklets, so honour demands of every man that he look no higher than the feet of the passing woman; and the behest is so faithfully observed that on the rare occasions when an Indian woman may need to undergo the ordeal I have known her own brother to let her go unrecognised.

For one need not say that women do now and then slip out on foot at nightfall, accompanied by a maid bearing a lamp, to enjoy an hour's gossip in some neighbour's house. We are all familiar with the powers of criticism of quiet women who never strayed into the great world, or saw more than the view from their own thresholds would reveal. What is true in this respect of the Western cottage is true also of the Eastern zenana. Woman's penetration is everywhere the same. Her good breeding makes everywhere the same demands. On one occasion I had the misfortune to introduce into my Indian home a European whose behaviour caused me the deepest mortification. But the ladies sat on the case when she had gone, and gravely discussed it in all its bearings. Finally it was gently dismissed with the remark, "She was not well-born".

On another occasion I came in one evening at the moment of some distinguished friend's arrival. Such was the empressement of her reception, the warmth of the inquiries after her health, and so on, that I felt myself to be certainly an intrusion. But a quiet hand detained me when I would have slipped away. "Wait," said the Mother, "till I have finished, for I haven't the least idea who she is!"

There were, however, certain practical difficulties in the life. It had taken some time, in the first place, to discover a house that could be let to an English-woman; and when this was done, it was still a few weeks before a Hindu caste-woman could be found who would be my servant. She turned up at last, however, in the person of an old, old woman, who called me "Mother", and whom I, at half her age, had to address as "Daughter" or "Jhee". This aged servitor was capable enough of the wholesale Hoodings of the rooms which constituted house-cleaning, as well of producing boiling water at stated times for the table and the bath. For some reason or other she had determined in my case to perform these acts on condition that I never entered her kitchen or touched her fire or water-supply. Yet hot water was not immediately procurable. And the reason? We possessed no cooking-stove. I asked the price of this necessary article, and was told six farthings. Armed with which sum, sure enough, my trusty retainer brought home a tile, a lump of clay, and a few thin iron bars, and constructed from these, with the greatest skill, the stove we needed.

It took some days to set and harden, but at last the work was complete. Afternoon tea, prepared under my own roof, was set triumphantly before me, and my ancient "daughter" squatted on the verandah facing me, with the hot kettle on the stone floor beside her, to see what strange thing might come to pass. I poured out a cup of tea and held out the pot to Jhee for more hot water. To my amazement she only gave a sort of grunt and disappeared into the inner courtyard. When she came back, a second later, she was dripping with cold water from head to foot. Before touching what I was about to drink she had considered a complete immersion necessary!

How happy were those days in the little lane! How unlike the terrible pictures of the Hindu routine which, together with that of the Pharisees in the New Testament, had embittered my English childhood! Constant ablutions, endless prostrations, unmeaning caste-restrictions, what a torture the dreary tale had been! And the reality was so different! My little study, with its modern pictures and few books, looked out on the cheeriest of neighbours. Here, a brown baby, with black lines under his eyes, and a gold chain round his waist, carried in triumph by his mother or nurse; there, some dignified woman, full of sweetness, as a glance would show, on her way to the bathing-ghat;

again, a quiet man, with intellectual face and Oriental leisure; and, above it all, the tall palm-trees, with little brown villages and fresh-water tanks nestling at their feet, while all kinds of birds flew about fearlessly just outside my window, and threw their shadows across my paper as I wrote. The golden glow of one's first sensation suffuses it still. It was all like a birth into a new world.

One evening, as I prepared for supper, a sound of wailing broke the after-darkness quiet of the lane, and making my way in the direction of the cry, I entered the courtyard of some servants' huts, just opposite. On the floor of the yard a girl lay dying, and as we sat and watched her, she breathed her last. Hours went by, and while the men were away at the burning-ghat, making arrangements for the funeral-fire that would be over before dawn, I sat with the weeping women, longing to comfort them, yet knowing not what to say. At last the violence of their grief had exhausted them, and even the mother of the dead girl lay back in my arms in a kind of stupor, dazed into forgetfulness for a while. Then, as is the way of sorrow, it all swept over her again, in a flood of despair. "Oh!" she cried, turning to me, "what shall I do? Where is my child now?"

I have always regarded that as the moment in which I found the key. Filled with a sudden pity, not so much for the bereaved woman as for those to whom the use of some particular language of the Infinite is a question of morality, I leaned forward. "Hush, mother!" I said, "your child is with the Great Mother. She is with Kali". And then, for a moment, with memory stilled, we were enfolded together, Eastern and Western, in the unfathomed depths of consolation of the World-Heart.

•••

2

THE HISTORY OF INDIA AND ITS STUDY

Two types of empire have occurred within the last two thousand years: one the creation of the fisher-peoples of the European coastline, the other of the tribesmen of Central Asia and Arabia. In the one case, the imperialising instinct is to be accounted for by the commercial thirst natural to those whose place has always been on the prehistoric trade-route. It may be true as suggested, the salmon-fishery of Norway, with its tightly organised crew, giving birth to the pirate-fisher the Viking, and he to the Feudal System and immediate ancestor of all modern European Empire. A strong sense of unity precedes aggression, and the sense of unity is made effective through organisation is obviously easy to gain by the conquest of the sea, where captain as first mate, and second son, and where the slightest dereliction from militaray discipline on the part of one may involve instant peril of death to all. Thus the family gives place to the crew as the organised unit of the human fabric, and the love of hearth side and brood becomes exalted into that civic passion which can offer up its seven sons and with firm voice, "Sweet and seemly is it to die for one's country."

The second type is the pastoral empire of Central Asia and Arabia. Islam was the religious form taken by the national unification of a number of pastoral tribes in Arabia. The earliest associations of the Arabs are inwoven with the conception of the tribe as a civic unity, transcending the family unity; and the necessity of frontier-tribal relationships and courtesies at once suggests the idea of national inclusiveness and creates a basis for national life. On these elements were laid the foundation of the thrones of Baghdad, Constantinople, and Cordova.

In the far past, those shadowy empires whose memories are all but dead to man—the Assyrian, the Parthian, the Median, and some others; seem to have based their powers of aggression and co-operation on the instincts and associations of the hunters.

India, as she is, is a problem which can only be read by the light of Indian history. Only by a gradual and loving study of how she came to be, can we grow to understand what the country actually is, what the intention of her evolution, and what her sleeping potentiality may.

We are often told that Indian literature includes no histories. Even if this be true—we must remember that India herself is the master-document in this kind. The country is her own record. She is the history that we must learn to read.

In all that lies around us, we may, if our eyes are open, read the story of the past. The life we live today has been created for us by those who went before us, as the line of sea-weed on the shore has been placed there by the waves of the tides now over in their end and flow. The present is the wreckage of the past. India as she stands is only to be explained by the history of India. The future waits for us to create it out of the materials left us by the past, aided by our understanding of this our inheritance.

In history we want to be able to see not the thing that would be pleasant, but the thing that is true.

The great names of Indian history—Buddhism, Shaivism, Vaishnavism, Islam, mean something to one.

One of the master-facts in Indian history, a fact borne in upon us more deeply with every hour of study is that India is and always has been a synthesis. No amount of analysis, racial, lingual, or territorial will ever amount in the sum to the study of India. Perhaps all the parts of a whole are not equal to the whole. At any rate all the fragments which must be added together to make India, we have to recognise India herself, all-containing, all dominating, moulding and shaping the destinies and the very nature of the elements out of which she is composed. The Indian people may be defective in the methods of the mechanical organisation, but they have been lacking as a people, in none of the essestials of organic synthesis. No Indian province has lived unto itself pursuing its own development, following its own path, going its way unchallenged and alone. On the contrary, the same tides have swept the land from end to end. A single impulse has bound province to province at the same period, in architecture, in religion, in ethical striving. The provincial life has been rich and individual, yet over and above it all India has known how to constitute herself a unity, consciously possessed of common hopes and common loves. Thus in the pursuit of epochs and parts we must never forget the motherland behind them all.

The Indian mind can hardly help making questions of antiquity into partisan arguments. Perhaps this is natural, but in any case is it a great barrier to the popularising of real historical inquiry. The mind of the student ought to be absolutely open on the point of dates. As a matter of fact, the strictly historical period in India may be comparatively short, something less than thirty centuries, but there can be no differences of opinion as to the vast length of the total period of evolution. The oldest problems of the world's history have their field of study here. Those sociological inquiries that lie behind all history must be pursued in India. History proper only emerges when a certain group of people becomes sufficiently consolidated to carry on common activities in a direction and with a motive that we may call political. This is a stage that will be arrived at soonest by communities which are relatively small and compact and inhabit clearly defined geographical confines, on the frontiers of other populations not greatly unlike themselves in civilisation. Thus **Egypt, Nineveh, and Babylon could not arrive sooner than India on the historical stage in virtue of their very nearness to one another. But this does not necessarily mean that they could compete with her in actual age,** or in the depth of the tendencies making for their evolution. And in any case, **while these are dead, India lives influences of the world about her,** and sees before her, as the individual unit that her development has made her, a long vista of growth and perfection to be achieved.

The art and architecture of Egypt date from four thousand years before the Christian era. Crete had a story almost as early. Who shall say what was the age of Babylon? When all these were already mature, India was still a-making. A long childhood, say the biologists, is the greatest proof of evolutionary advancement. **Egypt, with her exceptional climate, made art and architecture the supreme expression of her national existence. India put her powers perhaps as long ago, into the dreams and philosophy of the Upanishads. Cities would have crumbled into dust, temples and carving would have succumbed in a few aeons to the revages of time. Human thought, written on the least permanent and most ephemeral of all materials, is nevertheless the most enduring of all the proofs of our antiquity.** Who shall say that we have not chosen the better part?

We can hardly dig so deep into the past as to come upon the time when in Egypt or Greece, or Crete, or Babylon the name of India had not already a definite sound and association. At the very dawn of history in Europe, her thought and scholarship were already held in that respect which is akin to awe. His old tutor in the fourth century before Christ begs Alexander to bring him an Indian scholar! There is no need for discontent in the Indian mind, if those activities of which the historic muse can take account, activities intertribal, international, political, began for her comparatively late. **India, alone of all the nations of antiquity, is still young, still growing, still keeping a firm hold upon her past, still reverently striving to weave her future out of the past.** Are not these things enough for any single people?

The sociological habit is essential also if we would be in a position to gauge the relations of India to the incomers from beyond her border. Few people know that in the in grained beginnings of human society woman was the head of the family, and not man. In certain nations the memory of this ancient time of mother-rule is still deeply. Others like the Aryans, have long ago passed out of it. And some fragmentary communities in the world remain still more or less on the border line between the two. Only a deep familiarity with the traces of these different phases can give us a real clue to the history of Asia. Only a grasp of that history will enable us to compute distances of time truly.

The history of common things and their influence on our customs is a study that follows naturally on that of human society. Much of this we can make out for ourselves. For instance, **we can see that the ass must be older than the horse as a beast of burden. Once upon a time the world had no steeds, no carrier, save this useful if humble servant of man. Let us dream for a while of this. Let us study the present distribution of the donkey and find out his name in various Aryan languages. The goddess Shitala rides upon a donkey,** because in that dim past out of which she comes, there were as yet no horses tamed by man. There was once no steed so royal as the milk-white ass, which is now relegated here to the use of dhobis, while numerous are the allusions to its use, and the glory there- of, in the older Jewish scriptures.

After the horse was once tamed, men would never have taken the trouble necessary to reclaim the ass, and from this alone we may judge of its great antiquity.

At the same time we may form an idea of the time and effort spent on the gradual domestication of wild animals when we read the reiterated modern opinion that the zebra cannot be tamed. In the story of the commonest things that lie about us we may, aided by the social imagination, trace out the tale of the far past.

Thus the mind comes to live in the historic atmosphere. The search for stern truth is the best fruit of the best scientific training. But the truth is not necessarily melancholy and Indian students will do most to help the growth of knowledge if they begin with the robust conviction that in the long tale of the motherland there can be nothing to cause them anything but pride and reverence.

●●●

3

INDIAN THOUGHT : A SYNTHESIS

When existence was not, nor non-existence,
When the world was not, nor the sky beyond,
What covered the mist? By whom was it contained?
What was in those thick depths of darkness?

When death was not, nor immortality,
When night was not separate from day,
Then That vibrated motionless, one with Its own glory,
And beside That, nothing else existed.

When darkness was hidden in darkness,
Undistinguished, like one mass of water,
Then did That which was covered with darkness
Manifest Its glory by heat.

Now first arose Desire, the primal seed of mind,
(The sages have seen all this in their hearts,
Separating existence from non-existence.)
Its rays spread above, around, and below,
The glory became creative.
The Self, sustained as Cause below,
Projected, as Effect, above.

Who then understood? Who then declared
How came into being this Projected?
Lo, in its wake followed even the gods,
Who can say, therefore, whence It came?
Whence arose this projected, and whether
sustained or not,
He alone, O Beloved, who is its Ruler in the
highest heaven knoweth,

(Rigveda)

I

Like all the finest things in the world Indian thought had remained till the year 1893 without a definition, and without a name. For the word Dharma can in no sense be taken as the name of a religion. It is the essential quality, the permanent, unfluctuating core, of substance—the man-ness of man, life-ness of life, as it were. But as such it may assume any form, according to the secret of the individuality we are considering. To the artist his art, to the man of science his science, to the monk his vow, to the soldier his sovereign's name, to each believer his own particular belief—any of these, or all, may be Dharma.

There is indeed another, and collective sense—somewhat akin to the English *commonwealth*, or, better still, perhaps, translated as *the national righteousness*—but even this does not connote a creed. It applies to that whole system of complex action and interaction, on planes moral, intellectual, economic, industrial, political, and domestic— which we know as India or the national habit. By their attitude to it Pathan, Mogul, and the Englishman, are judged, each in his turn, by the Indian peasantry. As head of this system,

Yudhisthira, the Indian Charlemagne, received the name by which the people know him to this day, of Dharma-Raja. And what this Dharma was, in all its bearings, is perhaps best laid down in the charge of the dying Bhishma to the future sovereigns of India, in the Mababharata.

It is clear that such a conception is very inadequately rendered by the English word "religion". It is clear also that to dissect out and set in order the distinctively religious elements in an idea so definite at its centre, and so nebulous at its edges—claiming thereby to have defined the religion of the Indian peoples—would be a task of extreme difficulty. It must have been in the face of just such problems that Max Muller exclaimed, "Ancient words are round, and modern square!"

As the forest grows spontaneously, of many kinds, each like all the others only in the common fact of the quest of light, and every plant having a complete right to regard its own as the chosen seed, so amongst the Hindu people, up to the twentieth century of this Christian era, grew faiths and creeds.

It is not difficult to understand the mental outlook that is expressed in **the namelessness of Hinduism. An immense people, filling a vast territory,** unconscious of the completeness of their boundaries, or of any sharpness of contrast between themselves and neighbouring nations, **were necessarily incapable of summing up their thought, to give it a name.** A knowledge of limits and of difference there must be, before there can be definition, and it is only when India sees herself reflected as a whole in the glass of a foreign administration and a foreign language that she can dream of limitation. Besides, in things religious, what was there that was not included within the Hindu area? If, crossing the Himalayas and reaching China and Mongolia men came in contact with unknown rites and superstitions, they could always supply parallel or analogy from their home life and association.

Strange and powerful goddesses were adored in China, But the worship of the Mother is so old in India that its origin is lost in the very night of time. What an age of common faiths that must have been that left us the Virgin Kanyi (Kanya Kumari) as tutelary deity of Cape Comorin, and Kwannyon, the Mother as the giver of all blessings, in Japan to this day! Who is to say which is older, Kari, the Mother-Queenof Heaven,of Chinese mythology, or Kali of Bengal? Even these conceptions, however, dating as they clearly must from the days of that matriarchate when nations and races were not yet differentiated—even these do not represent the earliest stratum of religious thought in India or in Asia.

All through the Old Testament, and throughout the story of the rise of Mohammedanism, we hear of "stones" as objects of worship. It is the black and mystic Kaaba, that is to this day the symbol of their divinity to all the peoples of Islam. And throughout India still there are races of working folk who ask no better symbol of divinity than rude stones, selected with some care possibly, and then set up, singly or in a row, perhaps in an enclosure, perhaps not, to be regarded henceforth as objects of reverence. The people who use these emblems—for they cannot be regarded as images—may be anything, from Shudras, or peasants, as I have seen them in the South, to Bhutias, or gipsy-like wanderers, as one meets with them in the Himalayas.

Everywhere in common life the miraculous elements are fire and light. And perhaps it is natural that oil, with its mystic power of leaping into flame, should be the characteristic offering in the worship of these stones. A Bhutia shrine will sometimes contain nothing but lamps. These are small and made of iron, like round-bowled dessert-spoons at right angles to the handle, which is a spike struck into the ground, and I have seen as many as sixteen or seventeen in one tiny temple. There was here neither image nor symbol other than the lamps themselves, and the pilgrim on leaving would tear off a shred of his garment, and tie it to a bush or a tree close by, there joining hundreds of tokens like itself of the wayfaring congregation whose spirits had met unseen in a common act of adoration. But the place, as is always the case with these peasant oratories, was where the view was finest, and the cry of the soul to commune with Nature most intense. Sometimes the sacred stones themselves are smeared with oil, for the very touch of the wondrous fluid that nourishes light seems to be holy.

To richer races in India only clarified butter is good enough for use in the service of the altar, and we of Europe require the great wax tapers. But can we not trace through all these a single common process of the sanctification of labour by the products of labour? "We worship the Ganges with the water of the Ganges, but we *must* worship," said a Hindu. Similarly, does the peasant dream of the sacred oil, and the pastoral Toda[1] worship his cow-bells. Is it not true that if all could be blotted out in a moment from the human memory, the Eucharist and the sanctuary-lamp from

1. Toda—An aboriginal tribe in the Nilgiris.

Christianity, flickering light and fragrant flowers from the Mussulman grave, oils and fruits and incense from the Eastern worshipper, it would only be to spring forth fresh again tomorrow—corn, wine, and oil to the peasant, scented gums to the lover of gardens; the Good Shepherd, the ideal of the herdsman; the ship of salvation, the hope of fisher-folk? What are mythologies after all but the jewel-casket of humanity, by means of which its wealth of dreams and loves and sighs in every generation becomes unperishing and imperishable treasure of the after-comers? The mystery of the birth of faith is about us always.

All the great Asiatic faiths—that is to say, the world-religions—would seem to have been born of the overflow of something that may be called tentatively the Aryan thought-power, upon the social and religious formations of earlier ages. Taoism in China, Zoroastrianism in Persia, and Hinduism in India, are all as three different applications of a single original fund of insight and speculation, and Islam itself has incorporated Sufism after reaching the Aryan region. Doubtless of all these India developed her share of the inheritance with the greatest freedom and perfection, but we recognise common elements in all alike.

II

As the basis of Indian thought rests deep in the very foundation of human evolution, so it has not failed, at each new point in the historic development, to add something to the great superstructure. The whole story of India may be read in a philosophic idea. The constitutional ceremonies of the kingdom of

Travancore contain clear indications of the transition from the matriarchate which was probably characteristic of the old Dravidian civilisation, to the patriarchate, which was Aryan. In the yearly village-worship of the heroic figures of the Mahabharata which is common throughout the South, we have what may be the effort of distant peoples to include themselves in the "Great India" of Bhishma, Yudhisthira, and the national Epics. The charge of country gun-powder which is fired off in the temples of the Southern Deccan on festival days **is sufficient evidence that orthodoxy was once aggressive, eager, absorbent of things new, fearful of nothing, and friendly to advance.**

It is a popular superstition that the East stands still. Children observe no motion of the stars. But the fact is that one generation is no more like another at Banaras than in Paris. Every saint, every poet, adds something to the mighty pile which is unlike all that went before. And this is quite as true of the thought expressed in the vernaculars, as of the all-dominating culture contained in the classic Sanskrit. Chaitanya in Bengal, the Ten Gurus of the Sikhs, Ram Das and Tukaram in Maharashtra, and Ramanuja in the South—each of these was to his own time as the very personification of the national philosophy, relating it again in its wholeness to the common life. Each such great saint appears to the people as the incarnation, the revelation, of themselves and their own powers, and the church founded by him becomes a nation. Thus arose the Mahratta Confederacy. Thus arose the kingdom of Lahore. And far away in Arabia, Islam formed itself in the same fashion. For the law that we are considering is not peculiar to India; it is common to the whole of Asiatic life. The Hindu world in its entirety, then, is one with the highest philosophy of Hinduism. The much-talked of Vedanta is only the theoretic aspect of that synthesis whose elements make up the common life. The most unlettered, idolatrous-seeming peasant will talk, if questioned, of the immanence of God. He recognises that Christianity is fundamentally true, because the missionaries are clear that there is but one Supreme. The question, What would happen could the nation be divorced for a single generation from knowledge of Sanskrit? is only another way of asking, What is the actual dynamic force existing at a given moment in the Hindu people? What are the characteristic ideas that are now an inbred habit, past the reach of authority to substantiate, or disaster to shake? It is given only to great events and to the imagination of genius to find the answer to such questions. Yet some indications there are, of what that answer might be.

Buddhism was the name given to the Hinduism of the first few centuries of the Christian era, when it precipitated in a foreign consciousness. What authority did it claim? What explanations did it give of the existence of the physical universe? Of the soul? Of evil? What did it offer to humanity as the goal of the ethical struggle? The answer to these questions will certainly have to be given in terms of ideas, or variants of ideas, derived from the pre-existent stock of Hinduism. And so, though the particular formulation may be regarded as heresy, the significance of its testimony on the point we are considering cannot be disputed.

It must be remembered that there never was, in India, a religion known as Buddhism, with temples and priests of its own order. There was a tendency towards popularising truths that had previously been regarded as fit only for the learned, and there was an immense unofficial enthusiasm for a towering personality, doubtless, and for the interpretations which were identified with him, even as there is in Bengal today for Chaitanya. There came also to be a vast imperial organisation, highly centralised, coherent in all its parts, full of the geographical consciousness, uttering itself in similar architectural forms in the East, and west of India, passionately eager to unify and elevate the people and to adorn the land.

Indian Empire was in full and living communication with China, Japan, Syria, and Egypt. It had traffic and commerce by land and sea. It sent abroad ambassadors, merchants, and missionaries. And within its own territories it made roads, planted trees and orchards, dug wells, established hospitals, and insisted on the cessation of violence even towards dumb creatures.

Just as the Protestant Reformation, releasing the mental energy of the people from thraldom to athoritative commentaries, has been the power within the rise of modern Europe, so the kernel and spring of the Asokan and succeeding empires was a similar assertion, not of the right of private judgement—this never required vindication in India—but of the equal right of every section of society to enter the super-social, or monastic, life. For we must not forget that, **in the East, enfranchisement is always primarily religious and moral, not political. Power, civic and national, is there amongst the direct effects of the higher consciousness, never its cause.** It is a man's right to renounce the world, and not manhood suffrage, which constitutes his equality with the highest.

This sudden realisation of the spiritual life in all parts of society at once conferred on every man under Buddhism, whatever his birth or position, the right to make his opinion felt, the strength to exercise his full weight of moral influence. The result was an immense consolidation and blossoming of nationality. Men felt that they walked on air. They were born to receive and pass on the great message of human brotherhood. They were to go out into all the world and preach the Gospel to every creature. What must not have been the faith and enthusiasm of the common people, when merchants, traders, and caravan-servants could suffice to make a permanent contribution to the religion of the powerful Empire of China? It was a great age, and only those who have seen the colossal fragments which remain of it to this day can form any idea of its wealth and vigour.

And yet Asoka's conversion had not been to a new religion, but only into the piety of his time. "I, King Piyadassi, beloved of the gods, obtained true intelligence ten years after my anointing." Hence the thing that we call Buddhism ends its career in India very gradually. He who has first visited Ellora[1] is surprised, on entering Elephanta,[2] to find the Buddha-like figure on his left to be Shiva, and the Triumph of

1. Ellora—Buddhist cave-temples close to the north-western frontier of Andhra Pradesh. The town of Rosa, containing the tomb of Aurangzeb, is close by; and the whole is a few miles from Daulatabad, the ancient Deogiri.

2. Elephanta—A series of cave-temples on an island in the Bay of Bombay, between the second and the seventh century.

Durga on his right. At Ellora itself there must be a gap of centuries between the cathedral-like caves of Tin Tal[3] and of Kailas[4]. Yet even there we see the solitary figure of the teaching or the meditating Buddha give place by degrees to a rich pantheon of devas and guardian kings. But the hope and delight that are expressed so freely in the architecture and sculpture, and in the cosmopolitan intercourse of the Buddhist period die away imperceptibly into the rich imagery of the Puranic age,[5] and the manifold social and political problems of Shankaracharya and the age of chivalry.

The common tendency of Brahmins and Yogis had been to hold out the emancipation of the whole nature through self-discipline as the goal of endeavour. This doctrine came to be regarded in a loose way as characteristically Hindu. The Buddhist conviction was, on the other hand, that the same goal was to be reached, not so much by a gradual ripening of the self, as by ceasing from the illusion of egoism. Nirvana, not Mukti, became the watchword. The fact that these two ideas are related to each other as the obverse and

3. The Tin Tal—A cave-temple at Ellora which consists of three tiers or storeys. Hence its name. The most perfect of the non-Brahmanical structures.

4. Kailas—The most ornate and modern of all the cave-temples at Ellora. Cut with marvellous elaboration out of solid rock.

5. The Puranic age—The Puranas are the third class of Hindu sacred literature, the first being the Vedas and Upanishads, and the second the national Epics. They consist of a series of books of very mixed character, of which the representative specimens were written between the sixth and twelfth centuries. Hence this period is spoken of as the Puranic Age.

reverse of a coin, cannot have escaped the contemporary mind. But its own generation must have given a more antipodal value to the divergence than is obvious to Western thought at the present day. It would seem to them to include all possible theological differences, and it is not unlikely that this fact contributed largely to the belief so explicitly stated in the Gita, and so markedly Indian, that all religions express a single truth.

In the period of the Upanishads, the conception of Brahman—the one real appearing as many—had been reached. This implies the doctrine of Maya, or the illusion of things, as popularised under Buddhism. It is clear that in this theory. the whole question of the origin of evil is put aside. Evil and good are alike shadows on the wall, cast by our sense of personal convenience in magnified and distorted form. The saints recognise neither pain, insult, nor self-interest, being swallowed up in the joy of God.

The cyclic manifestation of the Cosmos—never created, but eternally self-existent, self-destroying, self-repeating-was another idea sown broadcast by Buddhist teachers. Here we have an interpretation that is significant of the immense scientific energy that has always gone hand in hand with Hindu religious speculation, making the spirit of research inherent in the spirit of devotion. Perhaps had orthodoxy offered the same resistance to science in the East that it did in the West, Indian investigation would have appeared more imposing today in the eyes of foreigners. **But the only thing that the Indian priesthood has conceived itself set to guard has been the social. It has opposed nothing save social aberrations.**

Knowledge has gone unhindered. And it will not be difficult to show that the much vaunted science of Moorish Spain was neither more nor less than the tapping of Indian culture for the modem world.

But perhaps the most significant of all points in the Buddhist propaganda is its assumption that the word of the Blessed One Himself is all-sufficient authority. Hinduism recognises only one proof, and that is direct perception. Even the sacred writings give as their sanction the direct perception of saints and sages, and the Vedas themselves declare that man must reach beyond the Vedas. That is to say, the books allege as their authority that realisation out of which they were written. The Jains refuse the authority of the Vedic texts. But there is less divergence between them and other sects of Hinduism than would appear on the surface. Common language and the historic acceptance of the race alike, lead up to the last great pronouncement on the subject—"By the Vedas no books are meant. They mean the accumulated treasury of spiritual laws discovered by different persons in different times."

"It is Veda," we say in India of a statement which we perceive to be profoundly true. It is held in a general way that there are two classes of scripture, one Vedas, the other Puranas. Puranas are characterised by containing stories of the creation and destruction of the world, tales of the life and death of holy persons and Avatars, accounts of their miracles, and so on. These elements are commonly mixed up, but can easily be disentangled. Thus, when the Christian Gospel says, "Thou shalt love the Lord thy God with all thy heart and with all thy soul," it speaks Veda; but when it says, "Jesus was born in Bethlehem of Judea in the days of

Herod the king" it is only a Purana, and may contain some elements of error.

Some of the greatest of French and English thinkers hold that the history of the West is made into a unity by the evolution of science and its progressive application to life, from the sixth century before Christ to the present day. These thinkers maintain that Greece, Imperial Rome, and the Catholic Church have been the three integral formative influences of what we call the European mind. To the student of Oriental history it appears equally clear that **the history of Asia is that of a single living organism, of which India may be taken as the heart and focus**. Regarded thus, in relation to its surroundings, the culture to which we give the name of Indian thought becomes likewise a unity, as clear, as continuous, as consistent in its development as is the evolution of the scientific idea in the West. Considered as an appanage of Europe, India is meaningless; taken in and for herself, and for that to which she rightly belongs, it need not surprise us if we find her the essential factor of human advance in the future as in the past.

India is the heart of Asia. Hinduism is a convenient name for the nexus of Indian thought. It would appear that it takes some thousand to fifteen hundred years to work out a single rhythm of its great pulsation. For this is about the period that divides the war of the Mahabharata from Buddha, Buddha from Shankaracharya, and Shankaracharya from Ramakrishna, in whom the immense pile reaches the crowning self-consciousness. Of the long pre-historic evolution that went to the building up of Mahabharata, Great India, the heroic age, we can say little, for nothing is left to us, save the legend of Sita and Rama, out of the night of time.

Yet we know that this period must have been long. Three thousand years seem not too much, if enough, to allow. Behind this again loom up the millennia spent on the tableland of Central Asia, that head-water of world-civilisation where Aryan man entered the patriarchate, and closed the account of his first combat with Nature, having tamed the beasts, learned the use of tools, domesticated corn and fire, produced the fruit-trees, and divided the week. Of the sublime dreams, the poetry and song with which he consoled himself during those ages of herculean struggle, the fragments known as the Rig-Veda still remain. And we learn therein how broad was his outlook upon Nature, even as that of the mind that declared, "And the evening and the morning were the first day." How long did it last? Was it ten thousand years? Were there another five thousand before the war of Mahabharata ...However this be, the enthusiasm of succeeding periods strikes us as extraordinary.

There is no question that the characteristic product of the civilisation that succeeded the Great War was the forest-universities, notes of whose sessions have become the Sutras and Upanishads. But we must not forget also that during the same period the Vedas were written down, and the searching scrutiny of society initiated which was later to result in those accumulations of reverent and sympathetic interpretations now known to us as the Laws of Manu.

It is only with difficulty that we realise the sense of vastness to which the thinkers of this period strove to give expression. **The Celt strives ever towards the**

infinite of emotion. The Hindu, in the same way, cannot rest content, short of the infinite of thought. We see this, even so early as the hymns of the Rig-Veda. "When darkness was hidden in darkness, undistinguished, like one mass of Water," opens the great Anthem of Creation. Still larger is the sweep of the Upanishads: "They that see the Real in the midst of this Unreal, they that behold life in the midst of this death, they that know the One in all the changing manifoldness of this universe, unto them belongs eternal peace—unto none else, unto none else." **The Vedas were the capital with which Aryan culture began its occupation of India, and these immense and subtle generalisations of the Upanishads represent the first achievement of the national mind in its new place.** Surely this is the secret of the striking fact in Indian history that all great eras of rejuvenescence, such as Shankaracharya's, and even minor movements of reconstruction like Guru Nanak's, and Ramanuja's, have had to go back to the forest Sutras and place themselves in structural continuity with them. In this light we begin to suspect that the war of the Mahabharata itself represents the apparent exhaustion of Vedic inspiration at the end of the first period, and the restoration of pristine vigour by force of Krishna's personality.

The twilight of Indian forests in the pre-Buddhistic age is resonant, to the historic ear, with chants and prayers. But the succeeding epoch leads us into the busy life of villages and cities. For the ballads and songs of the people are crystallising now into the great Epics. Their religious activity—stirred by the sublime spectacle of a life that represents the whole of Upanishadic culture, the national dream in its completeness—occupies itself with gathering together, and weaving into a whole, all the religious ideas innate amongst the masses, and those peculiar to the Indian environment. There is a sudden accession of focus given to such practices as pilgrimage and relic-worship, and Brahmin intelligence is more or less unconsciously preoccupied with the interpretation of images, symbols, and rituals, in relation to those truths which had been the first realisation of the race. The distinction and larger scope of this Buddhist period lay to a great extent in its political, commercial, and sub-religious elements, in letters, arts, and sciences.

Certain evils must have come in the train of the ideas then elaborated, essential as they were to prove themselves in the long run to the completed fabric of Hinduism. We can understand that monastic notions may have attracted too much of the national energy out of the safe paths of domestic virtue, with a tendency to bring about not only the depletion of family life, but the disintegration of morality itself. No doubt it was at this time, and to meet this error, that the song of the ideal sang itself so clearly, first through the lips of Kalidasa, in his "Birth of the War-Lord", and again, in the final recension of Ramayana, as the love of Sita for Rama, that glorified wifehood, before which the renunciation and faith of the cloister grow pale.

From the point of view of purity of doctrine, we can believe, too, that the very breadth of the welcome extended to religious ideas of all kinds, especially in the closing centuries of this age, had led to the undue emphasising of the popular notions, to the inclusion of an unnecessary multiplicity of symbols, and possibly to the interpretation of symbols already existing in rude or gross ways.

But agitation against abuses has never been the method of Hinduism. Rather has the faith progressed by lifting repeatedly in moments of crisis the banner of the highest ideal. Already, in the era we are considering, this organic law of the national genius, the law of the Avatars, was well known. "Whenever the Dharma decays, and when that which is not Dharma prevails, then I manifest myself. For the protection of the good, for the destruction of the evil, for the firm establishment of the national righteousness, I am born again and again." So says the Bhagavad-gita-and never was any prophecy more conclusively vindicated than this, by the appearance of Shankaracharya, early in the ninth century after Christ.

This wonderful boy—for he died at the age of thirty-two—was born at the end of the eighth century, and had already completed a great mission when most men are still dreaming of the future. **The characteristic product of Oriental culture is always a commentary. By this form of literature the future is knit firmly to the past, and though the dynamic power of the connecting idea may be obscure to the foreigner, it is clearly and accurately conveyed to the Eastern mind itself.** The whole of Confucianism is contained in a commentary on the I Ching or Book of Change, and European Protestantism might almost be described as a special kind of commentary on the Christian sacred literature. The Sanskrit Sutras lend themselves to critical writing, and even demand it, in a special degree: for the word Sutra means thread, and is applied to works which are only the main line of a given argument, and require expansion at the end of every sentence. This literary convention obtains in all Oriental countries, and must date from the period when the main function of writing was to assist memorising. Obviously, by writing a new commentary on a given Sutra, the man of genius has it in his power to re-adjust the relationship between a given question and the whole of current opinion. Hence it is not surprising to find that the masterpiece of Shankaracharya's life was a commentary on the Vedanta-Sutras.

The problems which faced the Indian mind during his lifetime, with the single exception that the country was then rich and prosperous, must have been curiously like those of the present day, and it is difficult to avoid the conclusion that in his eyes they assumed national dimensions. Religious practices had lost their primitive simplicity, and also perhaps their compelling power. Ideas as to national and unnational **(for the word "orthodox" was but the Asiatic word for "national")** were conflicting and confused. Men lived much in the thought of the recent sectarian developments of the faith, and tended to lose sight of its austere imperative, pointing to the highest realisation, of its antiquity, and its close-knit continuity. Lakshmi, Goddess of Fortune, was one of the chief objects of worship. Sects and kingdoms alike had lost their sense of mutual solidarity. Never perhaps was an Asiatic people nearer precipitating itself on a purely secular development.

At this moment the whole of the national genius awoke once more in Shankaracharya. Amidst all the brilliance and luxury of the age, in spite of the rich and florid taste of the Puranic period, his soul caught the mystic whisper of the ancient rhythm of the Vedic chants, and the dynamic power of the faith to lead the soul to super-consciousness, became for him the secret of every phase of Hinduism. He was on fire with the love of the Vedas. His own poems have something of their classical beauty and vigour, and his books may almost be described as chains of quotations from the most piercing and comprehensive sentences of the Upanishads, to which he has contributed links and rivets.

Shankaracharya wandered, during his short life, from his birth-place in the South as far as the Himalayas, and everything that he came across in his travels related itself to the one focus and centre, in his mind. He accepted each worship, even that from which he was at first adverse, but always because he found that the great mood of One-without-a-second was not only the Vedic, but also the Puranic goal. This is the doctrine that he expresses in his twelve epoch-making commentaries, especially in his crowning work, the commentary on the Vedanta-Sutras. And this idea, known as the Advaita Philosophy, constitutes, for the rest of the Hindu period, the actual unity of India.

Western people can hardly imagine a personality such as that of Shankaracharya. In the course of so few years to have nominated the founders of no less than ten great religious orders, of which four have fully retained their prestige to the present day; to have acquired such a mass of Sanskrit learning as to create a distinct philosophy, and impress himself on the scholarly imagination of India in a pre-eminence that twelve hundred years have not sufficed to shake; to have written poems whose grandeur makes them unmistakable, even to the foreign and unlearned ear; and at the same time to have lived with his disciples in all the radiant joy and simple pathos of the saints—this is greatness that we may appreciate, but cannot understand.

We contemplate with wonder and delight the devotion of Francis of Assisi, the intellect of Abelard, the force and freedom of Martin Luther, and the political efficiency of Ignatius Loyola; but who could imagine all these united in one person? Subsequent critics have painted Shankara-charya as the persecutor of Buddhists. Inasmuch as he asserted a co-ordination of mythologies and doctrines, instead of preaching a single exclusive method of salvation; inasmuch as to him the goal was a positive, and not a negative affirmation; and in so far also as he insisted upon the worthlessness of ritual apart from philosophy, of worship without illumination, he may be taken as the enemy of one school or another. It is almost unnecessary to add that this enmity was purely controversial in its character, and to Buddhists of the Northern School, a clearer historic knowledge will reveal him as the very opposite of a persecutor, as, rather, another example of the race of inspired religious teachers to which their own apostle, Nagarjuna, belonged.

Buddhism as a whole, with the succeeding Puranism, had been the creation of the lay mind, the creation of the people. The work of Shankaracharya was the relinking of popular practice to the theory of Brahman, the stern infusion of mythological fancies with the doctrine of the Upanishads. He took up and defined the current catchwords—Maya, Karma, reincarnation, and others—and left the terminology of Hinduism what it is today. At the same time, we must not neglect to remind ourselves that in all this, if he had been other than the expression of that which it was the actual tendency of the race to formulate, he would not have found the scope he did. The recognition of a great man is as essential a factor in his history as his own power and character. His complete appropriation by his nation only shows that he is in perfect unison with its thought and aspiration.

The great tide of vigour that emanated from Shankara-charya swept round India by south, west, and north, in a spiral curve. Ramanuja, Madhavacharya, Ram Das and Tukaram, the Sikh Gurus and Gauranga, were all in turn its products. Wherever it touched the Mussulman consciousness, it created, chiefly by means of contest, a well-centred nation. Where it did not come in contact with Mohammedanism, as in the extreme South, this spiritual energy did not succeed in evoking a nationality. And where it did not lead to definite fighting, as in Bengal under Chaitanya, the sense of national existence remained more or less potential. Thus the advent of Islam into India during the post-Shankaracharyan period cannot be regarded as a revolutionary invasion, inasmuch as under the new power there was no ioss of Asiatic modes. New arts of luxury were introduced, but the general economic system remained undisturbed. India received a more centralised government than had been possible since the Asokan Empire, but no new forces came into operation, tending to reduce her own children to the position of agricultural serfs or tenants.

Nor have the clearness and self-consciousness that its definition has added to Hinduism in any way tended to impair its inclusiveness. For the personality that the nineteenth century has revealed as the turning-point of the national development is that of Ramakrishna Paramahamsa, whose name stands as another word for the synthesis of all possible ideals and all possible shades of thought. In this great life, Hinduism finds the philosophy of Shankaracharya clothed upon with flesh, and is made finally aware of the entire sufficiency of any single creed or conception to lead the soul to God as its true goal. Henceforth, it is not true that each form of life or worship is tolerated or understood by the Hindu mind: each form is justified, welcomed, set up for its passionate loving, for evermore. Henceforth, the supreme crime for the follower of any Indian sect, whether orthodox or modern, philosophic or popular, shall be the criticism of any other, as if it were without the bounds of "the Eternal Faith". "Man proceeds from truth to truth, and not from error to truth," becomes in future the formula that constitutes belief.

At last, then, **Indian thought stands revealed in its entirety—no sect, but a synthesis; no church, but a university of spiritual culture—as an idea of individual freedom, amongst the most complete that the world knows.** Certain conceptions, such as Maya, Karma, and reincarnation, popularised by Buddhism, and Mukti or the beatific vision, sown and broadcast alike by Shankaracharya and the Sufis, are characteristic of large areas. But they are nowhere and in no sense regarded as essential. For it is as foreign to the genius of Hinduism to require an oath of conformity to any given religious tenet whatever, as it would be to the habits of an Oxford don to require adherence to the doctrines of Plato as against those of Aristotle. It would thus appear that the reforming sects of the nineteenth century itself, have to the full as good a right to call themselves Hindu as the most orthodox priest of Shiva, or the most learned Sanskrit pundit.

●●●

4

THE WHEEL OF BIRTH AND DEATH

The crucial feature of the Greek conception of life was the dramatic distinction which it made between will and the conditions with which will had to cope. Just as surely as our birth on the planet Earth gives us a place, definite, however infinitesimal, in the solar system, relating us in our degree to all that occurs within the orbit of the farthest satellite, so it is clear that our position, geographically, ethnologically, historically, upon that planet, places us from the beginning at definite points on lines of cause and effect, to which, as human beings, we can but exercise the function of acceptance. This not-to-be-refused, which modem science calls natural law, was simply to the Greek an unexplained and unexplored Necessity or Fate.

To the ancients, a curse, for example, was no exercise of the volition of the speaker. It was in no sense a threat. Our own more frivolous use of the word is a case of degradation by the death of a conception. To the old Greek, as indeed to the Hindu and the Norseman, a curse was entirely a prophecy. It was pronounced by way of warning or revelation that upon a certain act results would be found to follow. Apollo perceives that if Laios begets a son, disaster will result. He does not determine that it shall be so. Evidently, will is regarded as free up to a certain point, or we should not have the alternative imagined, of begetting no son. But to Oedipus and his children there is no alternative; he and they have been born in that circle of destiny where they can only fulfil the lot marked out.

This fact the Greek mind appears to accept without further inquiry. For it, overwhelming interest attaches, not to an analysis of the nature and conditions of fate, but to the spectacle of the human will in spiritual conflict with it. This spectacle is the theme of the whole of Hellenic tragedy. The Christian doctrine of grace introduces something confused and miraculous into the European idea of life, and for centuries the pursuit of the knowledge of things as they are is thwarted by a supernatural metaphysic of things as they ought to be, and are not. With the Renaissance, however, the intellect of Europe springs back sharply to the Greek position. Macbeth and Othello are in some ways as completely Hellenic as anything of Aeschylus. Temptation is once more placed outside a man; true and false incentives are inextricably blended; and the will is shown as the mere plaything of its own blindness. On these points, and in, the feeling of vastness with which he covers his subject, Shakespeare's delineation is all Greek.

In Macbeth, it is true, a sense of ethical suffering somewhat blurs the outline. But nothing dims the perfect beauty of Othello. Untortured by misgiving its heroic figures move from the dawn of their love to the noontide of supreme vindication of its purity in death. The particular problem is not antique. Its delicacy of tint is somewhat modern, but in simplicity and grandeur, in the conviction that life is a mere straw swept along on the current of necessity Othello is an ancient drama.

One great difference between the Hellenisms of antiquity and of the Renaissance lay in the fact that organisation was at the disposal of the modern. Isolated genius writes dramas, elaborates philosophies, or carves statues: organised genius produces scientific inquiry. In some sense modern science is nothing but the efficient development of the Aristotelian and Alexandrian elements of classical thought. The human will itself, however, is the one thing eternally baffling to human research. There is no crucible in which it can be melted. All science, therefore, resolves itself into the old problem of the Greek dramatist—the problem of due observation of the conditions which confront the will; and it is by a strictly logical development of the thought of the ancients—a thought which scarcely dreamt of any distinction between a man and his body—that we arrive at the modern conception of body-and-brain as the last and crucially important element of destiny.

Its naivete is at once the strength and weakness of European thought. The springs of modem fiction are still brackish with the salt of our enthusiasm about heredity. Recent talk of degeneration is little more than the bitterness left within a cup. Like every single truth mistaken for the whole, heredity would impose as great a bondage on the human spirit as any system of fatalism. Of what use is the fight against the weakness or ignorance of one's ancestors? What hope of victory over the taint that is in the blood? And yet, high over all law and all instruments rose, rises, and shall for ever rise, the human will, its brow bright with the sunshine of freedom, its foot on the foe that our subtle criticism had pronounced invincible, serene in the knowledge of its own power to defy a like heredity and the nature-of-things, and make for itself out of the web of failure the mantle of a supreme victory.

But this will so often seems asleep! Unaroused, or ignorant as a child, it has turned aside perhaps for every wayside flower, for any shining pebble, and in the hour of the crisis is simply missing. Or it may be that it suffers from some base intoxication of falsehood or desire, and has fallen down to kiss the feet of evil as though it were good, courting slavery and defeat as maidens to be caressed. Surely here, and here alone, is the crux of things, in the difference between the enlightened and the unenlightened will. Necessity is but the sum of the conditions. Heredity is but one, though the most critical, of those conditions. In the setting of the will itself towards bondage or towards freedom lies the secret of the unity of life.

There are thus three factors in the interpretation of human life, and it has been the distinction of Asiatic thought to have recognised all three. A profound certitude that cause must sooner or later be followed by effect, while effect has as surely been preceded by cause, gives to the Indian temperament an air of quiet resignation which is far from being the inactive fatalism so commonly supposed. For there is surely the difference of extremes between a dignified acceptance of things because they are unaccountable and not to be interfered with, and a similar dignified acceptance because they are so entirely accountable that events require no acceleration!

That India understands the doctrine of heredity is demonstrated by caste. There alone, amongst all the countries of the world, it has been held for ages an unpardonable social dishonour to allow the diseased or deformed or mentally alienated to marry. For such—the quietly enforced decree of caste has been always—no posterity. But more than this, the very meaning of the institution is, amongst other things, the attempt to develop still further the brain of the Brahmin, the hand of the toolbearer, and every form of expert faculty. It is true that it rejects the crossing of blood as a means to this end, but it looks to the cumulative influence of careful selection from generation to generation, to that of the occupational environment, and to the inheritance of the effects of clean feeding. The last is held specially important to the user of the brain: hence the Brahmin represents more than any other the fibre produced by countless generations of care in this respect, and the lower we go in society the less do we find of such transmission.

But the Indian comprehension of the nature of things and of heredity as complementary elements in the scheme presented to the will has never meant blindness to the last and most important consideration of all—the efficiency of the will itself. If this were not the determining factor, India would say, it would not be possible, as it is, to watch two brothers, with the same inheritance, the same material opportunities, and the same moral environment, journey, one to glory and the other to shame, by a common road. And if it were not also the ultimate standard of success or failure, the Greek story of Aristides, for instance, would lose all its pathos. For we all know how, when an ignorant man asked his help in casting his vote for the condemnation of Aristides, the great man first complied with his request, and then, on mildly inquiring its reason, was answered, "I am tired of hearing him called 'the just'."

Is it here, or in the story of Dives and Lazarus, that we catch a glimpse of inequality? Which is the crueller perplexing of our sense of justice—that one man receives wealth and another poverty, or that one cannot wish well, nor another ill?

The answer of India is not doubtful. There is one tool and only one, she says, that is finer than the most perfect human brain, and that is the tool of a noble intention. No more than other delicate instruments is this, she claims, immediately producible wherever we may wish to see it. Just as faculty grows from feeble and unrationalised to its perfection, just as organisms progress from minute and simple to large and complex, so must we suppose that will passes through all the stages of egotism till it reaches that illumination which we know as perfect charity. At each stage the possibilities of aspiration are limited, though they become less and less so as the goal is approached.

The whole Hindu outlook is thus critical and scientific. There is no longer a vague horrible something called Sin: this has given place to a clearly defined state of ignorance, or blindness of the will. Nor is this ignorance conceived of as a stationary or fixed quantity. So surely as trees grow and rivers seek the sea will it sooner or later give place to knowledge, in every human soul; and then a man's mere forgetfulness of his limited personality and its aims may look to others like nobility: to himself it will not even be apparent, lost in the larger yearning of more universal life. Thus a great and generous thought is like a position near the river-mouth to the water springing at the source, not by any means to be reached without traversing the complete distance.

The supreme good fortune possible to man would consist of a noble intention, joined to a great brain, joined to an external position of mastery and freedom—an advantageous point—that is to say, on some line of cause and effect. Such, we may take it, to Gautama the Buddha, was the opportunity of his birth. Most lives, however, represent every possibile degree, and combination of degrees, of the three conditions. We see the great position made the background of stupidity and meanness. We see the kind wish rendered futile by feebleness of intellect. Very occasionally there is no discord between person and circumstance; but now and again the discrepancy takes the acute form of the lion caught in the net, or the common criminal wearing an entperor's crown. Whence have these anomalies arisen? In what firm order do they stand rooted?

The Hindu mind seems always to have been possessed of the quiet confidence that all phenomena will yield themselves to a rational explanation. Since "that which exists is one", it is absurd to suppose an ultimate contradiction between the human reason and the universe. The mind that is normal and right amongst its fellows is normal and right in its relation to things. If we see and hear and taste, it is because in primal vibration there is something correspondent to sight and sound and the rest, of which our human sense has been the necessary outcome. Our faculty, that is to say, may be feeble, but we must assume it to be true. If thirty years of life can impress us with a sense of terrible duration, utterly disproportionate to their relative importance, it is because in the Absolute there is no passage of time, all the infinite eternities of consciousness lying in the Now. If human love can oppress us with a vastness undreamed of, suddenly opened before us, it is because in it we have approximated to a state which transcends all limit and all change. Whatever be the nature of the Real it must include, not exclude, consciousness. This being so, we must take it that the order of things as we see them—time, space, and causation—applies to life itself as naturally as to all that within the limits of life we perceive.

Our appearance here from birth to death is a simple case of the sequences that every moment of our stay brings to our notice. It is the effect of some cause which could no more have failed to find its fulfilment in time and space than the self-striking of a bird's wing could fail to be accompanied by flight. Everything, again, within the general effect, is a subordinate effect conditioned by its own subordinate cause. Physical, mental, and moral, are only terms denoting so many dimensions, as it were, within which the seed has germinated and come to its fruition.

So much for the effect. Do things, as we see them, give us any hint as to the nature of the cause? Yes, there is one force—the force ot desire—that we see at work daily, making, cherishing, gathering, action and its fruits. Without this as creative antecedent it will be found on examination that nothing that we know of comes to pass. Hence if life as a whole be regarded as but a phenomenon similar in kind to those which it encloses, we are impelled to the conclusion that of it also the efficient cause has been the human will.

We dreamed of ourselves as bodies. Falling into some strange error, we longed for the sweets of sense. And we awoke and, without knowing it, found ourselves in prison, there but to continue adding to the energy of those desires, each of which was already a fetter binding us the faster. Such is the Hindu interpretation of our presence here. Of what led to our self-deceit he attempts no account, conceiving that his right to a rational theory applies only to the phenomenal, meaning those things that are perceived within the play of reason.

Thus, life is a harvest reaped at birth. It is also the sowing of fresh harvests for the painful reaping of the future. Every act is as a seed, effect of past cause of effect to come—Karma. The unending wheel of birth and change and death. For the Hindu does not consider that a single life alone is to be accounted for. The very constitution of our minds forces on us the idea that phenomena are cycle; that appearances recur; that the starry Universe itself blooms and will wither like another flower. Clearly then the causes that have placed us here today must bring us again; must, in the circling of infinite ages, have brought us infinite times before. This is the doctrine of Reincarnation. Our ignorance now tells of a deeper ignorance in the past. The desires that burn within us are but our subjective apprehension of what is yet to be. For that which we long for must come to our hand. The Karma of each birth is only the harvest of our ancient wishes.

What the victim of desire so constantly forgets, however, is the twofold nature of things, and their constant state of flux. Good brings evil; wealth is succeeded by poverty; love is but a messenger sent before the feet of sorrow. In fact, the seeming benefits of material things are in reality scourges, sooner or later to lash the very back of him who drew them to himself. None, for instance, could be so puerile as to declare palaces, jewels, and horses as good in themselves, so that their chance possession now and again should be any compensation for the suffering of requiring them. It is little more exalted, says the Hindu, to claim love, intellect, and salvation, as necessities. The world of Maya consists of the perpetual alternation of opposites. Every desire carries its fulfilment, its decay, and its retribution hidden within itself. That what we would have we must first give, is the lesson of austerity.

The Karma of an individual, then consists of a given condition of taste or knowledge, a given physical equipment, and a given share of material fortune or misfortune. Taste sometimes rises to genius, or sinks to brutish appetite. The physical equipment may include a mathematician's brain, a violinist's hand, or a body tortured by perverse temptations. In any case, according to the theory, the will that has come to administer, earned exactly that endowment, and in this respect life is justly distributed. It is thought not unnatural that the soul of a Bach should seek incarnation in a family of musicians, since here it could best find the conditions it demanded. With regard to such matters, a vast lore has been accumulated, into which it is interesting to dip. There is a popular belief amongst Hindus that marriage is always contracted between the same two persons, and that the merit of either is divided equally with the other. However this may be, love at first sight—an occasional experience the world over—is held a sure proof of past friendship and acquaintance. Very perfect relationships, by which is meant, amongst other things, those that are complex in their quality, would be considered in the same way, to be long-rooted.

The religious life is one of the most fascinating subjects of speculation. It will sometimes happen that the stern ascetic in the midst of his austerities yields to, or at least harbours, some vain desire. This is enough to precipitate him once more into the world, where his position and power will be exactly equal to the severity of his past renunciations. He may thus very easily become a monarch, and it is believed that a faint memory of the religious habit often haunts the throne. **The great Akbar of Delhi told of such a reminiscence in his own case. He had been a monastic novice, and had fallen in love! When sovereignty was exhausted, however, he would return to his prayers and gain freedom, without another fall.** An impression of this kind about Queen Victoria was the real secret of the influence of her name in India—an influence, be it added, which would have been much deepened had she succeeded in abdicating some few years before her death, in order to devote the rest of her life to God.

We must remember, however, that the Oriental, born to the idea of reincarnation, rarely becomes so infatuated with it as to make it his sole dependence in interpreting life. He does not lose his head over it, as may one who hears of it for the first time. He is well aware that, on his own hypothesis, we are engaged in the sowing of seed, as well as the reaping of grain. He will not therefore attempt to explain every new introduction from an imaginary past. This life is to him but one measure in a long passage of music. The great majority of its tones gain all their beauty and meaning from the fact that they were prepared beforehand and will be resolved after, but some nevertheless are new. That we do not, as a rule, remember our pasts is, he argues, no disproof of their existence, since neither do we remember our birth and infancy.

It is this clearness of logical speculation that lends its terror to the Indian notion of existence. To the wise man, frankly, life is a bondage, and the only question how to be freed from it. Suicide cannot solve the problem. The reasons for this act may be frivolous or weighty. It is an instrument as much within a man's own power as the tools of his calling or the weapons of self-defence. Only, it offers no escape from the misery of existence. Can the school boy make progress in arithmetic by wiping from his slate the sum he could not work? Will not that particular difficulty recur whenever he would take an onward step, confusing, taunting, blinding him, till it is conquered? Even so is the lot of the suicide, thinks the Hindu. He desired to escape the rope of justice? Then in some future incursion into life it will become his Karma to stand on the scaffold and undergo the extreme penalty, for a crime he has not committed. He would flee from a dishonour he had not strength to endure? No coward's self-banishment shall suffice to save him. Sooner or later the ordeal must be met and faced. Or was it the abstract hatred of life that used his own hand to slay the man? Fool ! saw he not that the act was part and parcel of an extreme self-indulgence, and must bring its terrible consequence of exile from all that could make existence beautiful and blessed?

Desire, in short, is the ego-centripetal, the self-assertive, self-regarding force. The current must be turned out deliberately, not drawn inward. The passion for self must be destroyed in the thirst for service. Desire must be burnt to ashes in the fires of renunciation. Then, and then only, will there be escape from the incessant turning of the wheel. Then alone can the victim become the conqueror, and the slave master of the world.

This is the "cosmic suicide" of Schopenhauer, the much talked-of "pessimism" of the East. It is indeed a familiar conception to all Hindus, so familiar as to be an integral part of language. But it is hardly "pessimism". Does the prophecy of victory carry with it sadness? the certain promise of his freedom embitter the slave? There is a sense in which, if Hindu philosophy be not optimistic, it is difficult to know what the world means by optimism. Taking the doctrine of reincarnation as a whole, we find it so necessary to the theory of Maya that even the Buddhist formulation could not exist without some version of it. At the same time, a clear understanding of it is a valuable corrective of slipshod misconceptions as to the philosophy of illusion. That this involves no lazy intellectual uncertainty regarding phenomena we have seen, since the whole doctrine of Karma is based on the Hindu's implicit conviction of the entire calculableness of law. It cannot be too clearly understood that the argument of Maya is compatible with, and tenacious of, the severest scientific research, and tbat to Oriental thinking, only that man who has in his own person, by some method of self-discipline, achieved a realisation, compared to which all that we know through the senses is unreal, has a right to speak of the phenomenal universe as, to him, fundamentally an illusion. The effort to reach this vision remains, nevertheless, to the Oriental mind the one end and justification of existence, the one escape from the wheel of life; and mankind is for ever divisible into those who see and struggle towards such a goal, and those who are engaged in sowing the wind and reaping the whirlwind of Desire.

The battlefield of Kurukshetra lies silent these many centuries, yet still to the ear of the wise man it echoes the doom of Humanity in the terrible words: "Of that which is born, death is certain. Of that which is dead, birth is certain."

•••

5

LAW IN RELIGIOUS CONCEPTIONS

The essential differences between countries of the Asiatic and European types are as yet but little understood; and a main difficulty in the growth of an understanding is the absence of elements in the English language, embodying any wide power of social survey. The disciples of Auguste Comte have done much to popularise certain important words and conceptions, but the hearts of angels and the tongues of poets would be too little to meet all the necessities of the task.

The word theocracy, for instance, which is essential to an understanding of Asia, either territorial or historic, has but an ambiguous sound in English. To the learned Positivist it means "the social system built up on theism"; to the vulgar, it indicates some fabulous scheme of divine monarchy, such as is popularly attributed to Israel before the days of Saul, or to England in the dreams of Oliver Cromwell.

To persons thinking in the latter fashion, the two statements that India is a theocracy, and that it is occupied by the British Raj, seem incompatible. It is clear that only detailed and penetrative knowledge of concrete examples can build up in our minds such a conception of the essentials of a theocratic system as shall give us the power of handling the term as confidently and intelligently as we now feel capable of using more purely political expressions. And of such examples it will be found best to take the nearest first.

In the history of the world, the city of Rome occupies a unique position, as the Occidental cradle and battlefield of two opposing forces, the imperial and the theocratic, or, as one may prefer to call them, the European and the Asiatic ideas. For it was Rome that first imposed upon the West that notion of organised force which is almost all that is at present meant by the state-empire. And through all the feuds and disorders of the Middle Ages, it was the Roman impulse that was working itself out by the energy of barbarian peoples, to its perfect triumph in the nineteenth century. Caesar conceived, Napoleon completed, the imperial scheme. Alexander, as an individual, may have seen what they saw: but Greece was far too near to Asia, and his military designs could but evaporate before their time into mere learned observations and the exchange of interesting thought.

It was left to Rome to elaborate into fixity of precision that destiny which could not perhaps have been avoided by the peoples of a coast-line, kept militant by the daily conquest of nature, tempted to aggression by the very habits of their life. For empire in the European sense is a very different thing from the marauding hosts of the East going out to warfare headed by a commander of brilliant prowess. Rome instituted, and modern Europe has inherited, the idea of one people exploiting another, under rights strictly defined by law, with an appearance of order which would deceive the very elect.

The Caesars failed by the strength of the unassimilable elements which their empire had to meet. Napoleon failed because those whom he temporarily subdued were as strong to react in imitation as to be assimilated. Roman Empire is represented by some eight or ten emulous peoples and princes, all armed to the teeth, all bent on appropriating the world. But it is the Roman Empire still.

And yet Rome herself is the one character whose part in the drama is completely transformed. For no one yet thinks of her as the metropolis of the juvenile kingdom of Italy. To the imagination of humanity she is still the city of the Church. St. Peter's and the Vatican still form her central point. The Pope still rules. This contrast between her first and second selves is much more startling than the transition by which the brigand-chief becomes the sainted ancestor. Before it happened, it would have seemed far more absurd than it would be today'to propose to make the name of Oxford or Banaras a synonym for the vulgar competition of trade.

For Rome, the supreme, the invincible, has actually been conquered by the ideas of the East. The poor and the lowly have taken her by storm. Henceforth is she to be in Europe not the voice of domination, but of renunciation; not the teacher of aggression, but of self-sacrifice; royal in her rank and her prerogatives certainly, but far more deeply and truly the friend of the people than of kings. Henceforth, those who are in a special sense her children will live sequestered from the world, pursuing after poverty instead of riches, after self-mortification instead of self-indulgence; men and women apart, as in the Eastern household.

Every simple act that she enjoins will possess a sanctity out of all proportion to its intrinsic value. Her customs will become rituals. Her journeys will be pilgrimages. The simplest ordinances of life, administered by her, will now be sacraments. The expression of her forgiveness will be absolution; of her affection, a benediction. Her very rulers will claim no personal right to their high places, but will declare themselves simple executors of the divine will. "Servant of the servants of God" will be, to the thinking of the world, their proudest title.

In the eyes of the Church, henceforth, all .men are to be equal, at least until one has made himself a saint, and another Judas. The differences of rank established by the world are to be as nothing before her, and even ecclesiastical gradations are to be merely as conditions on which grace can work. Many of the saints will be humble and unlearned. Many a bishop will reach the lowest hell. Rank, at least theoretically, is nothing to Rome. Her children are all to be the sharers of a common supernatural life, of which a religious banquet is the token. A great responsibility is to rest upon them, of living worthily of the name by which they are called. Their life, as related to each other and to her, can be expressed only in terms of the exploration and manifestation of certain ideals, laid down broadly in authoritative writings, known as scriptures, and with less clearness and power in secondary writings and teachings, called traditions.

In other words, the imperial city has transformed herself into a pure theocracy. If we blot out the idea of birth by a sacramental rite, and substitute that of a chosen place and race, keeping everything else approximately the same, the Church is re-transmuted into anyone out of half a dozen Eastern countries—ancient EgyptJudea, Arabia, modern India—under the government of ,the religious idea. Here, too, the priesthood dominates all classes equally, and the priestly interpretation of life prevails—the very gifts one brings home from a journey are explained as temple-offerings. Here, too, the political system is extraneous: custom is sacred, so that a grammar of habit takes the place of legislation; men and women live apart; merit is the sole real condition of social prestige; and so on.

It is due to the purely natural character of the great complexus, that we have in India the—to us so extraordinary —spectacle of a society handed over to the power of a priesthood, without in any way losing its sense of the universal sacredness of learning and freedom of thought. In the case of Rome, where an artificial system was created on the basis of a foreign experience, the 'crude temper of the old imperialism betrayed itself primarily against mind and thought, which it conceived as the legitimate sphere of its authority. **In Catholic Europe, a man might scarcely venture to believe that the earth moves; must apologise for enjoying the cosmic speculations of La Place; could hardly study Plato without grave suspicion. In India, atheism itself might be preached on the very steps of the temple.** All that the people would demand of the preacher would be sincerity.[1] In Christendom, knowledge has been so

1. The Charvaka system of philosophy, one of the orthodox schools, is a purely agnostic formulation. I have myself met a Charvaka on a pilgrimage. His statements of belief sounded like mockery of the people about him. The word "orthodox" here only means that, by adopting Charvaka doctrines, a man did not cease to be called a Hindu.

much feared that men have again and again suffered torture and death for no other crime. **In India, knowledge has always been held to be beatitude. Abundance of words, in every Indian language, testify to the honour paid to scholars.** Persian and English books are held as sacred as the Sanskrit. And we should seek in vain, throughout history and language, for any trace of limitation imposed, or suggested to be imposed, upon the mind of man.

Even the vexed question of the right of literature to reveal more than is permitted to conversation, was foreseen long ago and settled in a flash of wit by the legislator who, writing of defilement by the touch of the mouth, makes three exceptions, in favour of "the beaks of birds, the lips of women, and the words of poets".

In fact, opinion is so free that religious propaganda is actually discouraged by Hinduism, lest zeal, outrunning discretion, prove mischievous to society. **"A man has a right to hold his own belief, but never to force it upon another," is the dictum that has made of India a perfect university of religious culture,** including every phase and stage of thought and practice, from that of the kindergarten, where all is concrete, to that of the higher research student, who has direct visualisation of the solutions of problems which most of us cannot even understand.

But freedom of thought in the East has not been the prerogative of religion alone. The deeper we go into the history of Hindu philosophy, **the more perplexed we are that with its obviously scientific character, it should never have created a scientific movement of the prestige and eclat of that of the**

West. Patanjali,[2] who wrote his great psychology in the second century B.C., was obviously a physiologist, studying the living body in relation to that nervous system which in its entirety he would call the mind. The action and interaction of the living neuro-psychosis is a question which modern science, content with a more static view of human structure, has hardly yet ventured to tackle; and students of Patanjali cannot be controverted if they hold that when it is reached, it will only be to corroborate the ancient investigation step by step.

But a still more interesting feature of Patanjali's work lies in the fact that **it is obviously the final record of a long research, carried out, not by a single individual, but by a whole school, experimenting continuously through many generations.** Each man's labour was conditioned by the fact that he had no laboratory and no instruments outside his own body, and there can be no doubt that life was often sacrificed to the thirst for knowledge. **The whole, therefore, is like a resume of two or three centuries of the conclusions of some English Royal Society, or some French Academy of Sciences, dating from two to three thousand years ago.** And we must remember that, if the terminology of this old science has a certain quaintness in our ears, this is probably not greater than that which our own talk of forces and molecules, of chemical affinities and sphygmographic records, would have, if it were suddenly recovered, after a lapse of two thousand years, by a new civilisation, stationed, say, in Mexico.

2. Patanjali wrote "Yoga Aphorisms". "Raja-Yoga" by Swami Vivekananda is a translation of this work, with a compilation from some of Patanjali's commentators.

What is true of the psychology is equally true of Indian mathematics, astronomy, surgery, chemistry. The Oriental predilection for meditative insight is an advantage in the field of mathematics, where deduction is a necessity. But at the same time its fundamental solidity and originality are shown by the fact that highly abstruse problems are stated by Hindu thinkers in concrete, and even in poetic terms. And it will be remembered that less than a hundred years ago, De Morgan[3] celebrated the solution at sight of certain hitherto uncompleted problems of "Maxima and Minima", by a young Hindu called Ram Chandra.

The law of gravitation itself was enunciated and discussed by Bhaskaracharya in the twelfth century. And the antiquity of the Sanskrit word Shunya, for nought, together with the immemorial distribution of the system all over the country, conclusively proves that our decimal notation is Indian, and not Arabic, in origin.

How is it, then, we repeat, that a more imposing scientific activity has not been the result of a faculty so undeniable? Many considerations may be adduced in explanation. There is a vast international organisation of scientific effort in Europe today, operating to make an incomparable sum of results. Ancient India knew what was meant by scientific co-operation, but by organisation scarcely. And no one nation, working alone, could have produced the whole of what we know as modern science, or even one division of it. Ancient Greece gives us the first word on electricity. What a

3. De Morgan died 1871. Pere Gratry and George Boole were other distinguished mathematicians deeply aware of their indebtedness to Eastern systems.

leap from this to Volta and Galvani. Where, again, had these been without tbe German Hertz, the French Ampere, the Hindu Bose? And then Italy for a second time takes up the thread of inquiry, and produces the apparatus for wireless telegraphy.

Again, we must remember that in Europe today we have renounced almost everything for science. Art and letters are almost at a standstill. In these departments—at least, in every country outside France and Russia—we are living almost entirely on the treasures of the past. In religion we see the same superficial eclecticism, the same absence of genuine contemporary impulse. But India never was in this position. Side by side with the learned man, speculating or experimenting on the secrets of nature, the builders were raising the village temple, the shuttle flew to and fro in the loom, the clink of the tools was heard in the brass smithy, the palace pundits busied themselves with their collection of ancient texts, the saints poured forth the rapture of their souls, the peasant waked and slept in the good company of nature, rice field and palm tree, cattle and farmstead. Faith, art, and industry lived on undisturbed.

After all, is it not possible that we deceive ourselves? The true secret of our elimination of every other intellectual activity in favour of science—is it really the depth of our enthusiasm for knowledge, or is it not rather our modern fever for its mechanical application? How far is the passion for pure truth unimpaired by commercial interests? How far is our substitution of specialisms for synthesis conditioned by finance merely? When our utilitarian ingenuity draws nearer exhaustion, when the present spasm of inventive ability has worked itself out, then, and not till then, will come the time for estimating the actual profundity and disinterestedness of our scientific ardour. Will our love of knowledge continue to drive us on to a still deeper theoretic insight, or will our investigations languish in our hands, lingering on as a mere fashion in learning, even as Aristotle lingered on through the Middle Ages? Till such questions are nearer finding their answer, we are in no position to assume that the present period is, or is not, ultimately scientific.

Meanwhile, in India this danger of a mercenary science was always foreseen, and viewed with perhaps an exaggerated horror, so that from the beginning the disciple has been required to seek knowledge for its own sake, renouncing all ulterior motive. The value derived at the present stage of development from incorporating a progressive science in a progressive civilisation was thus lost; although we must remember that in a very real sense such a transition, shorn of its lower elements, has occured in the East from prehistoric times, whenever new plants and animals were to be domesticated, or new tools invented. On the other hand, it is still open to India, facing the actual conditions of the modern world, to prove that the innate capacity of her people for scientific work and inquiry has been in no way lessened by this long abstention from its vulgar profits.

In spite, nevertheless, of the relative non-development of natural science in India, it is the perfect compatibility of the Hindu religious hypothesis with the highest scientific activity, that is to make that country within the present century the main source of the new synthesis of religion for which we in the West are certainly waiting. Several nations cannot suddenly come into contact by the use of a common language without a violent shock being given to their prejudices in favour of local mythology. Such an occurrence was inevitable in English-speaking countries under present circumstances, and has been accelerated, as it happens, by the agnosticism born of scientific activity.

Christianity, moreover, has been further discredited by the discovery that its adherents possess no ethics sufficiently controlling to influence their international relations, and finally by that worship of pleasure which an age of exploitation necessarily engenders. Thus neither the sentiment of childhood, the reasoning of theology, the austerity of conscience, nor the power of idealism, has been strong enough to maintain the creed of the West against the assaults to which the age has seen it subjected. Everything seems to be going through a transition. Social morality, intellectual formulas, legal and economic relationships, all have broken loose from their old moorings, and are seeking for readjustment. The first agony of the loss of belief is now over; but it has only given place to a dreary hopelessness, a mental and spiritual homelessness, which drives some in whom heart predominates into the Church of Rome, while others in whom the faculties are more evenly balanced, try to forget their need in social service, or in the intellectual and artistic enjoyments of an era of resumes.

Protestanti`sm has at last delivered herself of a genuinely religious product of the highest order, in that love of naked truth which finds its voice and type in modern science. For all other forms of non-Catholicism are more or less compromises, mere half-way-houses on the road to this. But, even in this, the environment of spirituality and the communion of saints are apt to be left behind with the Mediaeval Church. Is there no way to combine these things? Can the devotional attitude receive no justification from the clear and unbiased mind? Does religion, which has made so much of faith, want less than absolute conviction as its basis? Is that sentiment which has produced all the greatest art, and almost all the greatest conduct, to be relegated to the mental lumber-room, as, after all, only a superstition? Surely, if so, there is an eternal inharmony and divergence between the creative and the inquiring faculties of man.

But the very constitution of our minds forbids us to accept this paradox, It may be that we are no longer able to believe in the exclusive authenticity of any single religious system. But we are fast inclining to the opinion that even here there must be some observable sequence; that creeds and mythologies must be as genuine a product of the Unity-of-Things as the animals and the plants; that order and meaning there must be, in the one case as in the other. Instead, therefore, of a contemptuous disregard of all faiths as equally untrue, we are beginning to adopt to all alike an attitude of respect as equally significant.

Only in India has this recognition of law in religious conceptions ever been held in its completeness as a part of religion itself. Only in India have inspired teachers been able to declare that the name of God, being also an illusion, differed only from worldly things in having the power of helping us to break our bondage to illusion, while they, on the other hand, increased it. Only in India has it been counted orthodoxy to believe that all is within the mind, that the forms of gods are but objectifications of our own sense of what is best to be attained, that prayer is only the heightening of will. And, therefore, **it is from India that we shall gather that intellectualisation of belief which is to re-establish, in the name of a new and greater synthesis, our confidence in our own past.** In this new synthesis every element of our own thought must find a place—the conception of humanity and the worship of truth, of course because without these it would have no *raison d'etre*. But even the emotionalism of the negro must not go unplaced, uninterpreted, any more than that wondrous mood in which the explorer of knowledge finds himself launched on a vision of Unity that he dare not name. Neither the Catholic organisation of monasticism nor the Protestant (taken from the Mohammedan) inspiration of common prayer can be left out. There must be a religious consciousness strong enough to recognise the anguish of denial as its own most heroic experience, and large enough to be tender and helpful to the ignorance of a child.

In that other synthesis which grew up under the Roman Empire, all the Mediterranean peoples and those originally related to them found a part. The doctrine of immortality came from the desert; resurrection, mediatorship, and personal consciousness of sin from ancient Egypt; many elements from Persia and Syria; purity and asceticism from the Asokan Essenes; the basis of ethics to be transcended from Judea; the spirit of inquiry and the necessary feeling of an intellectual void from Greece, or at least from the Greek elements in Mediterranean society; the instinct of organisation from Rome; and the all absorbing renunciation and compassion for the world that alone can give sufficient nucleus for a new religion from one sweet central Personality, in whom each of these various hungers found its own Bethlehem—its house of bread.

Similarly, in the new up-growth of our own days, many preparatory influences now at work are to find fulfilment. All who have felt love of the disinherited and oppressed, all who have followed truth for its own sake, all who have longed to lose themselves in a paradise of devotion and been refused by the armed reason standing at the gate, all who have felt out for a larger generalisation, as they saw the faith of their babyhood falling away from them—all these have helped and are helping to build up the new consciousness, to make the faculty that is to recognise and assimilate the doctrine of the future. **But the evangel itself will be mainly drawn from India.**

And then, having thus renewed the sources of the world's inspiration, we may be pardoned if we ask: What of India herself? The Egyptian delivered up his whole treasure, and where is he now? Buried under many a layer of foreign invasion; tilling the soil as patiently and hopelessly as one of his own oxen; scarcely remembered, even as a name, by those who make so-called plans for the country's good, and are wakened only to a stupid wonder, as at the sound of something familiar from books, when they hear that to kill a cat today in the bazaar in Cairo would almost cost a man his life. The Jews produced Jesus, and what have they become? Pariahs and fugitives amongst the nations of men. Who remembers them with any feeling of gratitude for that which they have given? A miserable formula, "the Jews who crucified Him", has taken the place amongst the devout of any memorial of the fact that they created the language, the thought, the habits of life, and the outlook of righteousness, in which He assumed the garb of humanity.

Is something of this sort to be the fate of India? To give a religion to the world may be a sufficient proof that one's past was not in vain, but evidently it is no sort of safeguard for the future. The process by which the peoples of a vast continent may become mere hewers of wood and drawers of water has already begun, is already well afoot. Their indigenous institutions are all in decay. Their prosperity is gone. Some portion or other of the immense agricultural area is perpetually under famine. Their arts and industries are dead or dying. They have lapsed into mere customers for other men's cheap wares. Even their thought would seem to be mainly imitative. The orthodox is apt to tread the round of his own past eternally. The unorthodox is as apt to harness himself to the foreign present, with an equal blindness. In suicidal desperation, the would-be patriotic reiterate the war-cries of antagonistic sects, or moan for the advent of a new religion, as if, by introducing a fifth element of discord, the Indian peoples could reach unity. Nor does the education, at present offered, promise any solution of the problem. It is the minimum that is possible to the efficient clerk, and even that minimum is undergoing reduction rather than increase.

In spite of the absence of any theory of history that might elucidate the course of events in the East during the next two centuries, one truth reveals itself with perfect plainness. A nation becomes whatever she believes herself to be. She is made great, not by her relative superiority, but by her thought about herself. It becomes important, therefore, to ask: What conception of her own nature and power forms the inheritance of India?

As Roman Catholicism is but one element inhering in a great whole called Christianity, and as a man may well claim to be a good Christian without being a Catholic, so the religious system of Hinduism is only a fragment inhering in a vast social-industrial economic scheme called the Dharma, and a man may well and rightly be the servant of the Dharma, without calling himself a Hindu. It is this Dharma, in its large and non-sectarian activity, that determines the well-being of every child of the Indian soil. The word itself is an ancient name for national righteousness or national good. It is true that the Brahmin who bows before one who is not the rightful king is held many times accursed by Manu. It is true that **the Bhagavad-Gita is the only one of the world gospels that turns on the duty of fighting for the true sovereign against usurpers.** And yet it is also a fact that the person of the ruler is always a matter of singular indifference to the theocratic consciousness. It has been hitherto indeed a mere detail for military persons to fight out amongst themselves. The secret of so curious an attitude is reached when we discover that in the eyes of the Indian peasant, the sovereign himself is only the servant of the Dharma. "If he uphold it, he will stay: if not, he will have to go," they all say when questioned. Little do they dream, alas! that themselves and their children and their children's children may be swept into oblivion also by that same failure to uphold!

Thus, whoever was the master that an Indian statesman served—whether Hindu, Mussulman, or British sat upon the throne—it was the minister's duty, as the loyal and obedient child of an Asiatic race, to use all his influence in the best interests of his people and his country. It is this element in the national system that tends, with its great regard for agriculture, to rank the cow almost on a level with the human members of the commonwealth, making the Hindu sovereign forbid beef-eating within his frontiers. It was this that made a certain prince, in despair, hand over his salt-mines to the British Government, rather than obey its mandate to tax this commodity to his people, and thus derive personal benefit from their misfortune. It was this that made it incumbent upon many of the chiefs in the old days to provide, not only salt, but also water and fruit free to their subjects, a kind of "noblesse oblige" that has left the wayside orchard outside every village in Kashmir, till that favoured land is almost like the happy island of Avilion, "fair with orchard lawns, and bowery hollows crowned with summer sea".

It was this power of the Dharma to safeguard the welfare of its people, through a law as binding upon the monarch as upon his subjects, that brought about the immense network of custom which regulated the relief of beggars, the use of water, the provisioning of pilgrimages, habits of sanitation, distribution of grazing-lands, the forest rights of the peasant, and a thousand other matters of importance. The mere fact that the king's personal devotions were offered in a mosque would not interfere with his acceptance of the system, in any important measure. It was the language of rule, dominating all rulers alike, by every detail of birth and upbringing, and by the very impossibility of imagining any deviation. Hence it could never be more than a question of time till some new prince had assimilated the whole, and Mussulman, co-operated actively with Hindu in the great task of enforcing and extending the essentials of the common weal. We may regret, but we cannot condone, the strange indolence by which the Indian people have permitted themselves to lose sight of these national and civic responsibilities of their ancient civilisation, and become absorbed in its personal and domestic rites. Nor can we for one moment admit that this substitution of the trees for the forest deserves the name of orthodoxy—faithfulness to the Dharma.

It is, however, an essential weakness of theocratic rule that while it can tolerate any neighbour, it has no idea of dominating and unifying diverse elements round itself. The great mass of its subjects, too, see life indirectly through the nimbus of the supernatural. Instead of subordinating the priesthood in national affairs to the recognised leaders of the nation, exalting it only in its rightful capacity of influence upon the social and individual conscience, a theocracy is apt to require that its leaders move, encumbered by the counsels of the priests.

It was the Prophet's clear perception of these facts that gave its peculiar characteristics to Islam. He established a strong confraternity, and made subscription to a brief and concise formula its sole condition of membership. But Arab blood was comparatively unmixed and the greater part of Mohammed's work was done for him, in the close bond of consanguinity that united his central group. At one bound, and without any means save that power of personality which is the first demand of the theocratic method, he performed the double task of creating an all-absorbing consciousness of nationality, and carrying his people through the required emancipation of thought. To this day the great Semitised belt that divides Eastern Aryans and Mongolians from Europe, reminds us, whenever we look at the map, of the reality of his achievement. And the history of the origins of European learning remains to attest the enthusiasm of freedom which he conferred on the Saracenic intellect.

Geographical conditions impose upon India the same necessity of unification at all costs, and yet combine with other facts to make her the meeting ground of all races. Especially is this the case in modern times, when the ocean has become a roadway instead of a boundary. She is almost a museum of races, creeds, and social formations, some hoary with age, some crude with excessive youth. Thus her problem is vastly more difficult than that of Arabia before the seventh century. Yet she contains in herself every element of self-recovery.

If the fact had been open to doubt before, the British rule, with its railways, its cheap postage, and its common language of affairs, would sufficiently have demonstrated the territorial unity of the country. We can see today that India's is an organic, and no mere mechanical, unity. "The North," it has been said, "produces prophets, the South priests." And it is true that her intellectual and discriminating faculty, her power of recognition and formulation, lies in the South; that Mahratta, Mussulman, and Sikh, form her executive; while to Bengal, the country that has fought no battle for her own boundares falls the office of the heart, which will yet suffuse all the rest with the realisation of the vast inclusiveness of meaning of the great word "India". Historically the Indian unity is obvious. And if socially it appears doubtful, the country itself could set aside the doubt in an instant by grasping that intuition of nationality which alone is needed to give the spiritual impulse toward consolidation.

But the bare fact of an actual social, historical, and geographical unity, waiting for precipitation as a national consciousness, is not the only possession of India at the present crisis. She has a great past to return upon, and a clearly defined economy for model. Her traditions are unstained. There is no element of national life—art, poetry, literature, philosophy, science—in which she has not at some time been exceptionally strong. She has organised at least two empires of commanding character. **In architecture, three of the most imposing styles in the world have been hers—the Dravidian in the South, the Buddhist across middle India from Orissa to Bombay, and the Indo-Saracenic in the North.**

There can be little doubt that her next period will confront India with the necessity of introducing some community of ritual as between priest and people; and this of itself must create fresh architectural needs, a new architecture of the communal consciousness which would be sufficient to make the required appeal to the national imagination, and at the same time give the needed scope to the passion of democracy.

For in looking to the growth of a sentiment or nationality as the solution of Indian problems, we are, of course turning away from kings and priests, and appealing to woman and the people. A similar appeal, in the only form possible to the unmixed theocracy of that day, was made by Buddhism; and the whole history of India, from the Christian era onwards, is the story of the education of the popular consciousness, by the unifying and ameliorating influence of Hinduism, as it was then thrown open. **Today, if we adopt moral and intellectual tests as the criteria of civilisation, we can hardly refuse to admit that in such issues the East has been more successful than the West. In strength of family ties; in sweetness and decorum of family life; in widespread understanding of the place of the personal development in the scheme of religion as a whole; in power of enjoyment of leisure, without gross physical accompaniments; in dignity, frugality, continuous industry without aggressive activity; in artistic appreciation of work done and doing; and above all, in the ability to concentrate the whole faculty at will, even the poorest classes in India, whatever their religion, will compare favourably with many who are far above them in the West.** Such are some of the results of the Buddhist period.

The Mogul Empire fell into decay and failed, simply because it did not understand how to base itself on a great popular conception of Indian unity. It could neither assimilate the whole of the religious impulse of India, nor yet detach itself completely from it. Hence, as a government, it succeeded neither in rooting itself permanently, nor in creating that circuit of national energy which alone could have given it endurance. Nevertheless, it contributed invaluable elements to the national life of the future, and it is difficult to see how that life could hope to organise itself without its memorable preliminary experiment.

The foreign character of the English period produced, as its first effect, a sense of bewilderment and unrest, which gave birth to a hundred projected panaceas. There were social reformers, who thought that by a programme more purely destructive than they then realised, their Motherland would be best served. And while we may deprecate the form taken by their zeal, we can but admit that no other testimony could have been given to the living energy of the race which would have been so convincing. If Indian civilisation had really been stationary, as is so sapiently supposed by the West, the embers could hardly have leaped into such flame, at the bare touch of new ideas. If, on the other hand, the country had accepted the superficial theory and run agate in the endeavour to reform itself, we could not thereafter. have conceived of India as possessing sufficient depth and stability to make hope possible. Meanwhile, the reformers have not failed to bring forth fruit. They have produced groups of persons who represent what is valuable in Western thought and habits, without necessarily being denationalised, and they have demonstrated once for all the fact that India contains sufficient forces of restitution within herself to be completely independent of foreign advice and criticism.

Next came political agitators, who seemed to think that by entire deference to an alien idea their country would be saved. There can be no doubt that here also a valuable contribution had been made. The foreign idea can never save India—indeed, the use of the word "politics" in the present state of the country may strike some of us as a painful insincerity—but at the same time, the mastery and assimilation of the foreigners' method is an absolute necessity. The education of the people, also to a knowledge of their common interests, and the throwing of a net of friendship and mutual intercourse all over the country, are great services.

Outside social and political movements, again, there are a hundred emancipations and revivals of religious centres; all of which are noteworthy symptoms of inherent vitality. And still a fourth school declares that the one question of India lies in the economic crisis, and that that once surmounted all will be well.

At this moment, however, a new suspicion is making itself heard, a suspicion that behind all these interpretations—the social reform, the political agitation, religious movements, and economic grievances—there stands a greater reality, dominating and co-ordinating the whole, the Indian national idea, of which each is a part. It begins to be thought that there is a religious idea that may be called Indian, but it is of no single sect; that there is a social idea, which is the property of no caste or group; that there is a historic evolution, in which all are united; that it is the thing within all these which alone is to be called "India". If this conception should prevail, it will be seen that social, political, economic, and religious workers have all alike helped to reveal it; but it can never be allowed that the whole problem is economic, grave as the last-mentioned feature of the situation undoubtedly is. It is not merely the status, but the very nature and character of the collective personality of a whole nation, occupying one of the largest areas in the world, that has to be recaptured. In the days when ancient Egypt made an eternal impression on human civilisation, the personal belongings of her great nobles were no more than those of an Indian cowherd today. It was the sentiment of fraternity, the instinct of synthesis, the mind of co-ordination, that were the secret of her power.

The distintctive spirituality of the modem world depends upon its ability to think of things as a whole, to treat immense masses of facts as units, to bring together many kinds of activity, and put them in true relation to one another. This is the reality of which map, census, and newspaper—even catalogue, museum, and encyclopaedia —are but outer symbols. In proportion as she grasps this inner content, will India rise to the height of her own possibilities?

The sacraments of a growing nationality would lie in new developments of her old art, a new application of her old power of learnedness, new and dynamic religious interpretations, a new idealism, in short, true child of the nation's own past, with which the young should throb and the old be reverent. The test of its success would be the combining of renewed local and individual vigour with a power of self-centralisation and self-expression hitherto unknown.

But before such a result could come about, we must suppose the children of every province and every sect on fire with the love of the Motherland. Sikh, Maharatta, and Mussalman, we must imagine possessed each by the thought of India, not of his own group. Thus each name distinguished in the history of any part would be appropriated by the country as a whole.

The Hindu would prostrate himself on the steps of

the mosque, the Mohammedan offer salutation before the temple, the Aryan write the history of Islam with an enthusiasm impossible to those within its walls, the Semite stand forth as the exponent of India's heroic past, with the authority of one who sees for the first time with the eyes of manhood. For we cannot think that a mere toleration of one another's peculiarities can ever be enough to build up national sentiment in India. As the love of David and Jonathan, a love the stronger for distance of birth, such is that last and greatest passion which awakes in him who hears the sorrowful crying of the young and defenceless children of his own mother. Each difference between himself and them is a source of joy. Each need unknown to himself feeds his passion for self-sacrifice. Their very sins meet with no condemnation from him, their sworn champion and servant.

But has India today the hidden strength for such developments? What of the theocratic consciousness? What of warring religious convictions?

Whether or not she has adequate strength for her own renewal, only the sons of India are competent to judge. But it is certain that in the nationalising of a great nation, the two theocracies would reach, on the human side, their common flowering-point. Do not all kingdoms of God hold forth hope of a day when the lame shall walk, and the blind see, the leper be cleansed, and the poor have the Gospel preached unto them? The theocratic consciousness is never jealous of the social good, but profoundly susceptible of it. It seeks it, indeed, as its true goal. What of the theocratic consciousness, what of religion, should a day ever come to pass in which men discovered that divine revelations were meant to unite humanity, not to sunder it? Surely the question is hardly serious. The old orthodoxy of the Arab would still be the austerity of the Mohammedan. The ancient piety of the Hindu would still and for ever be the church of the devoted life. Yet both would have found new purpose and common scope, in the re-making of the Motherland.

Nevertheless, the question remains: The road is clear, but has India strength to follow it?

Jackals prowl about the buried cities and deserted temples of the Asokan era. Only a memory dwells within the marble palaces of the Mogul. Is the mighty Mother not now exhausted? Having given to the world, is it not enough? Is she again to rouse and bestir herself for the good of her own household? Who can tell? Yet in all impotence and desolation of the present, amidst the ruin of his country and the decay of his pride, an indomitable hope wakes still in the heart of the Indian peasant. "That which is, shall pass: and that which has been, shall again be," he mutters "to the end of time." And we seem to catch in his words the sound of a greater prophecy, of which this is but the echo:

"Whenever the Dharma decays, and Adharma prevails, then I manifest myself. For the protection of the good, for the destruction of the evil, for the firm establishment of The National Righteousnss I am born again and again."

●●●

6

BUDDHISM AND HINDUISM

Buddhism in India never consisted of a church but only of a religious order. Doctrinally it meant the scattering of that wisdom which had hitherto been peculiar to Brahmana and Kshatriya amongst the democracy. Nationally it meant the first social unification of the Indian people. Historically it brought about the birth of Hinduism. In all these respects Buddhism created a heritage which is living to the present day. Amongst the forces which have gone to the making of India, none has been so potent as that great wave of redeeming love for the common people which broke and spread on the shores of Humanity in the personality of Buddha. **By preaching the common spiritual right of all men whatever their birth, He created a nationality in India which leapt into spontaneous and overwhelming expression so soon as his message touched the heart of Asoka, the People's King.**

This fact constitutes a supreme instance of the way in which the mightiest political forces in history are brought into being by those who stand outside politics. The great Chandra Gupta, founding an Empire 300 B.C., could not make a nationality in India. He could only establish that political unity and centralisation in whose soil an Indian nationality might grow and come to recognise itself. Little did he dream that the germ of that Indian solidarity which was to establish his throne on adamantine foundations lay, (not with himself, but with those yellow-clad bhikshus who came and went about his dominions, and threaded their way through the gates and streets of Pataliputra itself. Yet time and the hour were with him. He builded better than he knew. **From the day of the accession of this Chandra Gupta, India was potentially mature. With the conversion of Asoka she becomes aware of her own maturity. Nothing appears more clearly in the mind of the great Asoka than his consciousness of the geographical extent and unity of his territory, and his sense of the human and democratic value of the populated centres.** We find these things in the truly imperial distribution of his decrees; in the deep social value of his public works-roads, wells, hospitals, and the rest; and, above all, in the fact that he published decrees at all.

Here was no throne-proud autocrat, governing by means of secret orders, but a sovereign, publishing to his people his notion of that highest law which bound him and them alike. Never did a monarch live who so called his subjects into his councils. Never was there a father who more deeply gave his confidence to his children. Yet without the work done by Chandra Gupta the grandfather and completed by Asoka himself in his earlier years, in the long-repented conquest of Kalinga, or Orissa, this blossoming time of true nationality, when all races and classes of Indian folk were drawn together by one loving and beloved sovereign, would not have been possible. Asoka owed as much to the political unity of India as to the wondrous vision which he had received from Buddha of all that it means to be a man, a human being, high born or low born, Aryan or non-Aryan.

But the question, "Of what spiritual confraternity did Asoka hold himself a member?" becomes here of considerable importance. To belong to a new sect does not often have the effect of opening a man's heart to all about him in this fashion. **Sects as a rule unite us to the few, but separate us from the many. And here lies the meaning of the fact that Buddhism in India was no sect. It was a worship of a great personality. It was a monastic order. But it was not a sect.** Asoka felt himself to be a monk, and the child of the monkhood, though seated on a throne, with his People as his church.

Similarly, to this day there may at any time rise within Hinduism a great Sannyasin, whose fully-enrolled disciples are monks and nuns, while yet he is honoured and recognised as the teacher or Guru by numberless householders. The position of the memory of Buddha as a Hindu teacher, in the third century before Christ, was not in these respects different from that of Shri Ramakrishna today, or that of Ramdas of Maharashtra in the seventeenth century. In the two last-named cases, however, the citizen-disciples, Grihastha-Bhaktas, have a well-defined background in which they inhere. Hinduism is long ago a virtual unity—though that fact may not yet have been realised and defined with its choice of religious systems to meet the needs of various types of character, and the great monastic Guru stands outside all as a quickening and spiritualising force, whose influence is felt in each alike. The citizen-Bhakta of Ramdas or Ramakrishna remains a Hindu.

In the days of Asoka, however, Hinduism was not yet a single united whole. The thing we now know by that name was then probably referred to as the religion of the Brahmanas. Its theology was of the Upanishads. Its superstitions had been transmitted from the Vedic period. And there was as yet no idea that it should be made an inclusive faith. It co-existed with beliefs about snakes and springs and earth-worship, in a loose federation which was undoubtedly true to certain original differences of race.

With the age of Buddhism all this was changed. The time had now come when men could no longer accept their beliefs on authority. Religion must for all equally be a matter of the personal experience, and there is no reason to doubt the claim made by the Jainas, that Buddha was the disciple of the same Guru as Mahavira. We know the age of a heresy by the tenets it contradicts, and in repudiating the authority of the Vedas, Jainism proves itself the oldest form of non-conformity in India. And in the same way, by its relative return upon Vedic thought, we may find in Buddhism an element of reaction against Jainism. Only by accepting the Jaina tradition, moreover, as to the influence which their Gurus had upon Buddha, are we able to account satisfactorily for the road taken by Him from Kapilavastu to Bodh-Gaya through Rajgir. He made his way first of all to the region of the famous Jaina teachers. If, again, there should be any shred of truth in Sir Edwin Arnold's story (presumably from the Lalita-Vistara) that it was at Rajgir that He interceded for the goats, the incident would seem under the circumstances the more natural.

He passed through the city on His way to some solitude where He could find realisation, with His heart full of that pity for animals and that shrinking from the thought of sacrifice, which was the characteristic thought of the age, one of the great preoccupations, it may be, of the Jaina circles He had just left. And with His heart thus full, He met the sacrificial herd, marched with them to the portals of Bimbisara's palace, and pleaded with the king for their lives, offering His own in their place. Whether this was actually so or not, it is certain that one of the great impulses of the day lay in the rebellion against the necessity of the Vedic sacrifice; one of its finest sincerities, in that exaltation of the personal experience which made it seem natural to found on it a religion.

That a man's religious convictions must be the result of his own private realisation of truth is an idea so old in India as to lie behind the Upanishads themselves. But that such a realisation had a right to be socialised, to be made the basis of a religious sect, is a principle which was first perhaps grasped by the Jainas. It is this decision, thus definitely arrived at and clearly held, that accounts for the strength and certainty of Indian thought to this hour. :For the doctrine that direct perception is the only certain mode of proof, and that all belief, therefore, rests on the direct perception of competent persons, is here unshakable; and it is easy to understand how such an attitude, on the part of a whole nation, exalts the individual thinker and the mind of genius.

The world is now so familiar with the spectacle of the religious leader going out from amongst his fellows and followed by all who think with him, to found some sect which is to be even as a new city of the human spirit, that it can hardly think itself back to the time when this was a thing unknown. In the age of the Vedas and Upanishads, however, the spectacle had not yet been seen in India. The religious teacher of those days lived retired in the forest clearings and gathered round him, not a sect, but a school, in the form of a few disciples. **Jainism, with its sudden intense revolt against the sacrificial idea, and its sudden determination to make its pity effective for the protection of dumb animals, was the first religious doctrine to call social forces to its aid in India;** in other words, it was the first organised sect or church, and by forming itself it invented the idea of sects, and the non-Jainas began to hold themselves in some sort of unity round the Aryan priesthood.

Buddha in his turn accepted from Jainism its fearless pity, but not contented with the protection of the dumb creature, added to the number of those to be redeemed man himself, wandering in ignorance from birth to birth, and sacrificing himself at every step to his own transient desires. He realised to the full the career of the religious teacher as Jainism had made it possible, yet the doctrine which he preached as the result of his personal experience was in all essential respects identical with that which had already been elaborated in the forest Ashramas of the Upanishads, as the "religion of the Brahmanas." It was in fact the spiritual culture of that period brought into being and slowly ripened in those Ashramas of peaceful thought and lofty contemplation that pressed forward now to make the strength behind Buddha as a preacher. He declared that which the people already dimly knew.

Thus, by the debt which he owes to both, this Great Sannyasin, calling all men to enter on the highest path, forms the bridge between the religion of the Aryans, tracing itself back to the Vedas, and the religion of the Jainas, holding itself to be defiant of the Vedas.

Such was the relation of Buddha to his immediate past, which he himself, however, overtopped and hid by his gigantic personality. We have next to look at the changes made by him in the religious ideas of succeeding generations. Taking Buddha as the founder, not of a sect, but of a monastic order, it is easy to see that his social organisation could never be cumulative. There must in fact come a time when it would die out. No new members could be born into his fold. His sons were those only on whom his idea had shone—those who had personally and voluntarily accepted his thought. Yet he must have had many lovers and admirers who could not become monastics. What was the place of the citizen-Bhaktas, the Grihastha-devotees of Buddha? We obtain glimpses of many such in the course of his own life. They loved him. They could not fail to be influenced and indeed dominated by him, in all their living and thinking thereafter. Yet they could not go out in the life of the wanderer, leaving the duties of their station. He was their sovereign, as it were, monarch of their souls. But he was not their general, for they were not members of the army. That place belonged only to monks and nuns, and these were neither.

Whatever was the place of the citizen-Bhakta, it is clear that he would express in that place the full influence of the personal idea that Buddha represented. Not Indra of the Thousand Eyes, delighting in sacrifice, could ever again be the dream of the soul that had once loved Gautama. Calmness of meditation, light and stillness, detachment and knowledge, are now seen to be the highest powers of man. And this new realisation constantly reinforced by new admirers, will do its great work, not within the Buddhist Order, but outside it, in the eventual modification of some other system. The conscious aim of the Order as such will be to maintain its first condition of purity, truth, and ardour. The unconscious aim of the world without will be to assimilate more and more of the overflow of idealism that comes from within it, more and more of the personal impress left by One in whom all men's aspirations have been fulfilled. From this point we can see that the Order itself must some day die out in India, from sheer philosophical inanition and the want of a new Buddha. But its influence on the faiths outside it will echo and reaecho, ever deepening and intensifying.

Those faiths were, as we have seen, three in number-(1) Jaina; (2) Arya-Vedic; and (3) popular unorganised beliefs. It would appear, therefore, that the citizen-Bhakta would necessarily belong to one or other of the groups. Already Jainism must have been a force acting, as we have seen, to unify the Arya-Vedic and the popular unorganised beliefs, giving its first impetus, in fact, to the evolution of what would afterwards be Hinduism, and this process Buddhism, with its immense aggressiveness for the redemption of man, would greatly intensify. Yet the period would be considerable before this influence of the Buddhist idea would be sufficient to make itself perceptible in Hinduism, and its emergence, when that period was completed, might be expected to be abrupt.

My own opinion is that **this influence makes itself visible in the sudden advent of the idea of Shiva or Mahadeva to a dominant position in the national life. In tracing out the evolution of the Shiva-image, we are compelled, I think, to assume its origin in the Stupa.** And similarly, in the gradual concretising of the Vedic Rudra into the modern Mahadeva, the impress made by Buddha on the national imagination is extraordinarily evident. Stirless meditation, unshadowed knowledge, fathomless pity, are now the highest that man can imagine of the soul. And why? For no reason, save that Buddha had gone to and for forty years after the attainment of Truth and the print of his feet could by no means die out in India! The caves of Elephanta in the Bay of Bombay are a cathedral of Shiva-worships. They contain, moreover, not only an emblem of Shiva which may be more or less modern, but also a great many carvings. And none of these has a greater interest and importance than that on the left side of the entrance, a bas-relief of Shiva, wearing beads and tiger-skin, and seated in meditation. It is Shiva: it is not Buddha. But it is the Shiva of the transition, and as such it is most significant.

For hundreds of years, then, before this emergence of Shiva as the main Hindu conception of God (which for a time he was), devout souls had loved Buddha and hastened with a special devotion to give alms to Sadhus, without on that account suspecting for a moment that they were of any but the accepted Arya-Vedic household of faith. Less dependence on the great powers that dwelt beneath the mountain springs; less sense of the mystery of serpent and forest; an ever-deepening reverence for the free soul, for the Sadhu, for the idea of renunciation, this was all of which anyone was conscious. And yet in this subtle change of centres, history was being made; a new period was coming to the birth. Verily, those were great days in India between 500 B.C. and A.D. 200 or thereabouts. For the national genius had things all its own way, and in every home in the land the little was daily growing less, and the real and the universal were coming more and more prominently into view. Those were probably the days of Gitas made in imitation of the Buddhist Suttas. And this fact alone, if it be true, will give us some hint as to the preoccupation of the period with great thought.

"Thou that art knowledge itself,
Pure, free, ever the witness,
Beyond all thought and beyond all qualities,
To thee the only true Guru
My Salutation:
Shiva Guru! Shiva Guru! Shiva Guru!"

These words may be taken as the keynote of this first period in the making of Hinduism The national faith will form itself henceforth like a great white Sankha (conch-shell) coiled in broadening spirals about the Vedic pillar. The theological Ishvara believed in by the Brahmanas is referred to vaguely but conveniently by themselves and others at this time as Brahma. He is the God to whom the sacrifices are made. But in the presence of Buddha and the memory of Buddha a new and higher conception begins to prevail; and as time goes on, this higher conception takes name and form as Shiva or Mahadeva. **Hinduism is thus born, not as a system, but as a process of thought, capable**

of registering in its progressive development the character of each age through which it passes.

It follows, then, that **the heirs of Buddha-Bhakti, so to speak, in India, might be on the one hand Jainas, or on the other Shaivite Hindus.** These were the two churches whose children might be born as if in the shadow of Buddha. And it is in accordance with this that **we find Shaivism and Jainism subsequently dividing between them such places of Buddhist history as Banaras and Rajgir.**

●●●

7

BANARAS: SONG OF THE PAST

Even in great places we cannot always command the passive moments of rare insight. It was already my third visit to Banaras when I sat one day, at an hour after noon, in the Vishvanatha Bazar. Everything about me was hushed and drowsy. The Sadhu-like shopkeepers nodded and dozed over their small wares; here the weaving of girdle or scapulary with a Mantra, there a collection of small stone Shivas. There was little enough of traffic along the narrow footway, but overhead went the swallows by the invisible roadways of the blue, flying in and out among their nests in the eaves. And the air was filled with their twittering, and with the sighing resonance of the great bell in the Temple of Vishveshvara, as the constant stream. of barefooted worshippers entered, and prayed, and before departing touched it. Swaying, sobbing, there it hung, seeming as if in that hour of peace it were some mystic dome, thrilled and responsive to every throb of the city's life. One could believe that these ripples of sound that ran across it were born of no mechanical vibration, but echoed, here a moan, there a prayer, and yet again a cry of gladness, in all the distant quarters of Banaras; that the bell was even as a great weaver, weaving into unity of music, and throwing back on earth, those broken and tangled threads of joy and pain that without it would have seemed so meaningless and so confused.

A step beyond were the shops of the flower-sellers, who sell white flowers for the worship of Shiva across the threshold. Oh what a task, to spend the whole of life, day after day, in this service only, the giving of the flowers for the image of the Lord! Has there been no soul that, occupied thus, has dreamed and dreamed itself into Mukti (liberation), through the daily offering?

And so came to me the thought of the old minsters of Europe, and of what it meant to live thus, like the swallows and the townsfolk and the flowers, even in the shadow of a great cathedral. For that is what Banaras is—a city built about the walls of a cathedral.

It is common to say of Banaras that it is curiously modern, and there is on the face of it a certain truth in the statement. For the palaces and monasteries and temples that line the banks of the Ganges between the mouths of Baruna and Asi have been built for the most part within the last three hundred years. There is skill and taste enough in India yet to rebuild them all again, if they fell tomorrow. Banaras, as she stands, is in this sense the work of the Indian people as they are today.

But never did any city so sing the song of the past. One is always catching a hint of reminiscence in the bazars, in the interior, and in the domestic architecture. Here is the Jammu Chhattra for instance, built in the Jaunpur Pathan style, common in Northern India from the twelfth to the fourteenth centuries. Not far off again, we have a glimpse of a roof-balustrade that retains many of the characteristics of an Asokan rail, so clearly is it a wooden fence rendered in stone. I have seen a pillared hall too, in a house looking out upon the Ganges, that might almost have known the two thousand years that its owners claimed for it. And here in the hazar of Vishvanatha we are treading still, it may be, that very pathway through the forest that was followed by the Vedic forefathers, when first they saw the sun rise on the East of the great river, and offered the Homa (oblation) where the golden grate of Vishveshvara stands today, chanting their *rijks* in celebration of worship.[1]

Nothing holds its place longer than a road. The winding alleys between the backs of houses and gardens in European cities may, at no distant date, have been paths through meadows and cornfields. And similarly, in all countries, a footway is apt to be a silent record of unwritten history. But who shall recover the story of this little street, or write the long long poem of the lives and deaths of those whose feet have passed to and forth along its flagstones in four thousand years?

Truly the city, even as she stands, is more ancient than any superficial critic would suppose. It was here at Sarnath, in the year 583 B.C. or thereabouts, that the great message pealed out whose echoes have never died away in history: "Open ye your ears, 0 Monks, the deliverance from death is found!" And the importance which the Deer-Park thus assumes in the life of Buddha, both before and after the attainment of Nirvana, sufficiently proves its importance as the university of philosophy of its own age. Three hundred years later

1. The allusion here is not only to the Sanskrit Rik, but also to the early Norse *rijks* and *runes*.

Asoka, seeking to build memorials of all the most sacred events in the history of his great Master, was able, as the recent excavations show us, to make a tiny Stupa with its rail in some cell, by that time already underground, whose site had been especially sanctified by the touch of Buddha's feet.

We thus learn, not only that the Deer-Park of Banaras (so called, probably, because pains were taken to keep it cleared of larger game) was important in the year 583 B.C. and again in 250 B.C., but also that it was sufficiently a centre of resort throughout the intervening period to guarantee its maintenance of an unbroken tradition with regard to points of extremely minute detail. But it was not Sarnath alone that saw the coming and going of Buddha in the birth of the great enlightenment. Nor was it the Abkariyeh Kand alone that had already formed an important religious centre for ages before the early Mohammedan period. The very name of the Dashashvamedha Ghat and Bazar commemorates a period long enough to have included ten imperial sacrifices, each one of which must have represented at least a reign. Probably throughout the Pataliputra age, that is to say, from 350 B.C. to A.D. 528, Banaras was the ecclesiastical and sacrificial seat of empire. It contains at least two Asokan pillars, one in the grounds of the Queen's College, and the other, as we now know, at the entrance to the old-time Monastery of Sarnath. And we know with certainty that in the youth of Buddha it was already a thriving industrial centre. For the robes that he threw aside, perhaps in the year 590 B.C., to adopt the Gerua (ochre garb) of the Sannyasin, are said in many books to have been made of Banaras silk.

But this is in truth only what we might have expected. For the waterway is always in early ages the chief geographical feature of a country, and the position of Banaras at the northward bend of the river determines the 'point of convergence for all the foot-roads of the South and East, and makes her necessarily the greatest distributing centre in India. Thus **she constitutes a palimpsest, not a simple manuscript, of cities. One has here been built upon another; period has accumulated upon period.** There are houses in the crowded quarters whose foundations are laid, as it were, in mines of bricks, and whose owners live upon the sale of these ancestral wares. And there is at least one temple that I know of whose floor is eight or ten feet below the level of the present street, and whose date is palpably of the second to the fourth century after Christ.

If then we may compare large things with small, **Banaras may be called the Canterbury of the Asokan and post-Asokan India.** What Delhi became later to the militarised India of the Rajput and the Moslem, that Banaras had already been to an earlier India, whose eastern provinces had seen Buddha. At Sarnath the memory of the great Sannyasin was preserved by the devoted members of a religious order, either Buddhist or Jaina. At Banaras the Brahmanas laboured, as citizens and householders, to enforce the lesson that none ,of his greatness was. lacking in the Great God. The Shiva, clad in the tigerskin and seated in meditation like a Buddha, who is carved in low relief at the entrance to Elephanta in the harbour of Bombay, was the Hindu ideal of the later Buddhist period. And so the Vedic city, through whose streets had passed the Blessed One, became the sacred city of Shiva; and to make and set up his emblem there—the form in stone of the formless God—was held for long ages. after the same act of merit that the erecting of votive Stupas had so long been in places of Buddhistic pilgrimage. Nay, even now old Stupas. remain of the early Pauranika period, and early Shivas of a later phase of development, about the streets and ghats, of Banaras, to tell of the impress made by Buddha on an age that was then already passing away.

But **Banaras is not only an Indian Canterbury, it is also an Oxford. Under the shadow of temples. and monasteries cluster the schools and dwellings. of the pundits or learned Sanskritists,** and from all parts of India the poor students flock there to study the classics and ancient rituals of Hinduism. The fame of Nadia is in her Sanskrit logic, but that of Banaras in her philosophy and Brahmana lore. Thus **she remains ever the central authority on questions of worship and of the faith, and her influence is carried to all ends of India** by every wondering scholar returning to his own province.

It is a medieval type of culture, of course, carried out in the medieval way. It takes a man twelve years here to exhaust a single book, while under the modern comparative method we are compelled to skim the surfaces of a score or more in a single year. It follows that we have here a study of the contents rather than the relations of a given work; significance rather than co-ordination. But for this very reason the Banaras-trained scholar is of his own kind, secure in his type, as fearless in his utterance of that which he knows as those other medievalists in a modern ;world, John Bunyan and William Blake.

But in Banaras, as a culture-centre, even in the present generation, though it is fast vanishing, we have another extraordinary advantage to note. Being as she is the authoritative seat of Hinduism and Sanskrit learning, the city stands nevertheless, side by side with Jaunpur, the equally authoritative centre of Mussulman learning in India. She represents in fact the dividing line between the Sanskritic civilisation of the Hindu provinces and the Persian and Arabic culture of the Mohammedan. And consequently she still has members of a class that once constituted one of the most perfect types of national education in the world, elderly Hindu gentlemen who were trained in their youth not only to read Sanskrit literature, but also to read and enjoy what was then the distinctive accomplishment of royal courts, namely, Persian poetry. And the mind that is born of this particular synthesis—rendered possible in Banaras by the presence on the one hand of the Hindu pundit and the neighbourhood on the other of the Jaunpur *maulvi—is* not that of a great scholar certainly, but it is that of a member of the wide world, polished, courtly, and urbane. One of the most charming forms of high breeding that humanity has known will be lost with the last well-born Hindu who has had the old time training in Persian. Nor indeed can anyone who has seen modern and medieval culture side by side, as we may still sometimes see them in Asia, doubt that the true sense of literature is the prerogative of the medievalist.

Banaras, then, is an informal university. And like other universities of the Middle Ages, it has always supported its scholars and students by a vast network of institutions of mutual aid. It is no disgrace there for a boy to beg his bread, when love of learning has brought him a thousand miles on foot. Nor was it in medieval Leipzig, or Heidelberg, or Oxford. These are the scholars for whom our schools and colleges were founded. The wives of the burghers expected to contribute to the maintenance of such. And it is in Banaras, only food that is wanted. In the dark hours of one winter morning, as I made my way through the Bengalitollah to the bathing-ghats, I could hear in the distance the sound of Sanskrit chanting. And soon I came up to a student who had slept all night on the stone verandah of some well-to-do house, screened from the bitterest pinch of cold by carefully-drawn walls of common sacking, and now had risen before five to read by the light of a hurricane lamp and commit to memory his task for the day. Further on another studied, with no such luxuries as canvas walls and paraffin lamp. He had slept all night under his single blanket on the open stone, and the tiny Indian Batti (lamp) was the light by which he was reading now.

Here is love of learning with labour and poverty. It is obviously impossible for these to earn their bread in addition to performing the tasks imposed by their schools. The spontaneous benefactions of rich nobles and merchants were doubtless enough in the Middle Ages—when religious enthusiasm was high, and the problem still limited—to maintain the pundits in whose houses the students lived. But in modern times the institution of the Chhattras has grown up, and it is said that in the city there are three hundred and sixty-five of these. A Chhattra is a house at which a given number of persons receive a meal daily. Some give double doles. Some give to others beside Brahmanas. Many have been themselves the gifts of pious widows, and a few of kings. But that it is the duty of the city to provide food for her scholars all are agreed. Is not Banaras, to these children of Shiva, Annapurna the Mother, She whose hand is ever "full of grain"?

But Banaras is more than the precincts of a group of temples. She is more even than a university, and more than the historic and industrial centre of three thousand years. The solemn Manikarnika stands rightly in the centre of her river-front. For she is a great national Shmashana, a vast burning ghat. "He who dies in Banaras attains Nirvana." The words may be nothing but an expression of intense affection. Who would not love to die on those beautiful ghats, with the breath of the night or the morning on his brow, the sound of temple bells and chanting in his ears, and the promises of Shiva and memories of the past in his heart? Such a death, embraced in an ecstasy, would it not in itself be Mukti, the goal? "Oh Thou great Jnana, that art God, dwell Thou in me." Such was the vision that broke upon one who bent from the flower-seller's balcony to see evensong chanted by the Brahmanas round the blossom-crowned Vishveshvara. And never again can that mind think of God as seated on a throne, with His children kneeling round Him, for to it the secret has been shown that Shiva is within the heart of man, and He is the Absolute Consciousness, the Infinite Knowledge, and the Unconditioned Bliss. Which of us would not die, if we could, in the place that was capable of flashing such a message across the soul?

All India feels this. All India hears the call. And one by one, step by step, with bent head and bare feet for the most part, come those, chiefly widows and Sadhus, whose lives are turned away from all desire save that of a holy death. How many monuments of Sati are to be seen in Banaras, one on the Manikarnika Ghat, and many dotted about the fields and roads outside! These are the memorials of triumphant wifehood in the hour of its bereavement. But there are other triumphs. Clothed and veiled in purest white, bathing, fasting, and praying continually, here in the hidden streets of Banaras dwell thousands of those whose lives are one long effort to accumulate merit for the beloved second self. And if the scholar be indeed the servant of the nation, is the saint less? The lamp of ideal womanhood, burning in the sheltered spot at the feet of the image, and "not flickering", is this, or is it not, as a light given to the world?

Banaras, again, is an epitome of the whole Indian synthesis of nationality. As the newcomer is rowed down the river past the long lines of temples and bathing-ghats, while the history of each is told to him in turn, he feels, catching his breath at each fresh revelation of builded beauty, that all roads in India always must have led to Banaras. Here is the monastery of Kedarnath, the headquarters of the southern monks, which represents to the province of Madras all the merits of Himalayan pilgrimage. Here again is the ghat of Rani Ahalya Bai, the wonderful widowed Mahratta Queen, whose temples and roads and tanks remain all over India to witness to the greatness of the mother heart in rulers. Or behind this we may see the Math of Shankaracharya's Order, the high caste Dandis, whose line is unbroken and orthodoxy unimpeached from the days of their founder, early in the ninth century, till the present hour. Again, we see the palace of the Nagpur Bhonslas (now in the hands of the Maharaja of Darbhanga), connecting Banaras with the memory of the Mahratta power, and further on the royal buildings of Gwalior and even of Nepal. Nor is everything here dedicated to Shiva, Shiva's city though it be. For here again we come on the temple of Beni-Madhava, one of the favourite names of Vishnu. Even Mohammedan sovereigns could not submit to be left out. Secular science is embodied in the beautiful old Man-Mandir of Akbar's time, with its instruments and lecture-hall, and the Mussulman faith in the towering minarets of Aurungzeb's mosque.

But what is true of the Ganges front becomes still more clear when we pass behind and consider the city as a whole. Ranjit Singh made no separate building, but he linked Vishveshvara irrevocably with Amritsar, when he covered its roof with gold. Zemindars of Bengal, Sirdars of the Punjab, and nobles of Rajputana, all have vied with one another in leaving temples and shrines, charities and benefactions, dotted over the Pancha Krosha.

Or we may see the same thing industrially. We can buy in Banaras, besides her own delicate webs, the Saris of Madras and the Deccan alike. Or we may go to the Vishvanatha Bazar for the carpentry of the Punjab. We may find in the same city the brasswork of Nasik, of Trichinopoli, and ot the Nepalese frontier. It is there, better than anywhere else in India, that we may buy the stone vessels of Gaya, of Jabalpur, and of Agra, or the Shivas of the Narmada and the Shalagramas[2] of the Gumti and Nepal. And the food of every province may be brought in these streets, the language of every race in India heard within these walls.

On questions of religion and of custom, again, in all parts of India, as has been said, the supreme appeal is to Banaras. The princes of Gwalior dine only when the news has been telegraphed that the day's food has been offered here. Here too the old works of art and religion, and the old craftsmen practising quaint crafts, linger longest, and may still perchance be found when they have become rare to the point of vanishing everywhere else. Here the Vyasas chant authoritative renderings of the epic stories on the ghats. And here at great banquets food is still considered only secondary to the reciting of the scriptures. Surely it is clear enough that as in the Latin Empire of City and of Church the saying grew up, "All roads lead to Rome," so also in India, so long as she remains India, all roads, all faiths, all periods, and all historical developments will lead us sooner or later back to Banaras.

A city in such a position, possessed of such manifold significance, the pilgrim-centre of a continent, must always have had an overwhelming need of strong civic organisation. And that such a need was recognised in the city during the ages of its growth, we may see in many ways. No medieval township in Europe gives stronger evidence of self organisation than we find here.

"The medieval city," says the great European sociologist Kropotkin, "appears as a double federation: of all householders united into small territorial unions—

2. Round emblems of Vishnu

the street, the parish, the section—and of individuals united by oath into guilds, according to their professions; the former being a product of the village-community origin of the city, while the second is a subsequent growth, called into life by new conditions."

This is a master statement which can at once be applied here, if only we dismiss the European idea of labour as the main motif of this city's growth, and substitute the Indian equivalent of religion and learning. Labour is present here of course, and has flourished, as we know, in this spot, during at least three thousand years, but it has never reared its head to become a predominant and independent factor in the growth of Banaras. This central significance, this higher element in the federation, has been supplied here, by the presence of priests and pundits, monasteries and poets, bound to each other, not by professional oaths, but by the invisible and spiritual bonds of caste and tradition, and religious bonds—by Hinduism, in short. Not the craftsman, but the Hindu carrying the craftsman with him, has made Banaras what she is, and here in this city we have the picture of one of the finest things that the Indian faith—uninterfered with by foreign influences, and commanding the enthusiastic co-operation of the whole nation—could produce. It is no mean achievement. On Banaras, as it has made it, the Hindu genius may well take its stand. By the city of Shiva it may well claim to be judged.

It is, however, when we turn to the first element in Kropotkin's analysis of the city that we find Banaras to be most completely illuminated. In a pilgrim city, we cannot but think that some mutual organisation of householders for self-defence must have been a prime necessity. The policing of such a city was more than usually important. What were the arrangements made for sanitation, for ambulance, for hospital-service, for the clearing-out of vagrants? These things may not in the Middle Ages have been called by these names, but assuredly their realities existed, and such necessities had to be met. Householders united into small territorial unions-the street, the *para*. And is not Banaras filled with small courts and alleys, divided from the main streets by short flights of broad steps, each crowned by its own gate? Is it more than thirty or forty years since each of these had its own guard or concierge and was closed at night to be opened again in the morning? In many cases of course the massive doors themselves are now removed, but the pillars and hooks and hinges still remain to bear witness to their old function. In other instances they stand there still pushed back against the wall, and one pauses a moment as one passes to ask, "When was this last shut?"

These portals to each little group of important houses are a silent witness to the order and cleanliness of Banaras as the Hindu made it. Just as in Edinburgh, as in Nurnberg, as in Paris, so here also, the group of wealthy houses thus barred in at a certain hour after dark was responsible for the freedom of its own space from uncleanliness and violence. It must undertake the connection between its own sanitation and the underground sewage system of the city, which was similar in character to that of ancient Pataliputra. It must be responsible for the proper alleviation of such suffering as fell within its limits, and its members must duly contribute their full share to the common burdens of the city as a whole. But when we come to the gates of the *para* or section, of which some still remain guarded by their watchmen outstanding in the bazars, we understand the full importance to the medieval mind of the question of civic order and of a strong but peaceful civic defence. For here within these gateways, we find the shrines of Kala Bhairava, the divine Kotwal, who perambulates the city of Shiva night after night, with staff and dog, who is worshipped by sentinels and gate-keepers, and who has the supreme discretion of accepting or rejecting at his will those who fain would enter within the sacred bounds. Of the divine Kotwal every city watchman held himself as minister and earthly representative. And in this worship of Kala Bhairava, the Black Demon of Shiva, we may read the whole history of the civic organisation of Banaras in the Middle Ages.

The modern age was later perhaps in arriving here than elsewhere. But arrive it did, and its work when it came, here as elsewhere, was to multiply problems and to discredit the solutions that had been discovered by slow ages of growth. All that strong rope of self-defence, twisted of so many strands of local combination and territorial respon-sibility, with which Banaras had been wont to meet her own needs, was now done away. The communal sense was stunned by the blow, for the fact was demonstrated to it ad nauseum that it was itself powerless against strong central combinations of force. Thus the old self-jurisdiction and self administration of the civic group was banished. And at the same time the railways connected Banaras with every part of India, and made it possible to pour in upon her daily as large a number of diseased, infirm, and starving persons, as may once have reached her on foot or in boats in the course of a year. Thus a forest of needs has grown up in modern Banaras, of which the past generations with their common sense, their spontaneous kindliness, and their thrifty municipal management, knew nothing.

Poor working-folk come, when the last hope has failed them, trusting that the Great God will be their refuge in his own city. In the old days, when Banaras was a wealthy capital, these would have made their way to some house or *para* inhabited by well-to-do townsfolk from their own district, and through their kind offices work would sooner or later have been found. But now they find themselves amongst strangers. The music of temple-bells is the only sound familiar to them. Priests and fellow worshippers are alike unknown. And it may be that in the sanctuary-city they have but fled from one despair to another.

Or the poor student comes here to learn. In the old days he would have found house-room as well as food in the home of his Guru, or of some wealthy patron, and if he fell ill, he would have been cared for there, as a member of the family. Today the number of so-called students is great, and possibly amongst them the indolent are many. For certainly temptations must have multiplied, at the same time that the moral continuity of the old relation between distant homestead and metropolitan *para* has been lost. In any case, even amongst the most earnest, some of these poor students have, as we have seen, to live in the streets. And when illness overtakes such, there is none to aid, for there is none even to know. The Chhattras are certainly a wonderful institution, showing the unexpected power of this ancient city to meet the needs of her own children. But the Chhattras cannot offer home and hospital. And these also are sometimes needed.

And finally there is the case of the widowed gentlewomen who come to Banaras to pray for their dead. As with others, so here also there is in many cases but slender provision. And yet nowadays they cannot come to friends, but must needs hire a room and pay rent to a landlord. Nor can we venture to pass too harsh a verdict on the capitalist who evicts his tenant—though a woman and delicately nurtured -when the rent has fallen too long into arrears. For he probably has to deal with the fact on such a scale that the course is forced upon him, if he will save himself from ruin. More striking even than this is that fear of the police. which we find everywhere amongst the helpless, and which drives the keeper of the apartment-house to dismiss its penniless inmates when near to death, lest he should afterwards be arraigned in court for having stolen their provision!

Prostrate, then, under the disintegrating touch of the Modem Era, lies at this moment the most perfect of medieval cities. Is she to become a memory to her children after four thousand or more years of a constant growth? Or will there prove to be some magic in the new forces of enthusiasm that are running through the veins of the nation, that shall yet make itself potent to renew her ancient life-streams also?

•••

8

ELEPHANTA—THE SYNTHESIS OF HINDUISM

At a great moment in the history of India the caves of Elephanta were carved out of the living rock. A moment of synthesis it was that ages had prepared; a moment of promise that would take millenniums to fulfil. The idea that we now call Hinduism had just arrived at theological maturity. The process of re-differentiation had not yet begun. The caves of Elephanta mark perhaps its greatest historic moment. In all religious sects the conflict of opinion is determined more by the facts of history and geography than by opposing convictions. What then were the sources, geographic and historic, of the elements that make up Elephanta?

The caves themselves were meant to be a cathedral. So much is apparent on the face of things. **Traces of palace, fortifications, and capital city must certainly be discoverable in their immediate neighbourhood.** On another island several miles away is the Abbey of Kanheri with its Chaitya hall and its 108 monastic cells, each two of which have their own water-supply; its bathing tanks, and tefectory or chapter floors on the mountaintop. **Kanheri was a university: Elephanta was a cathedral: and both were appanages of some royal seat.**

How splendid is the approach through pillars to the great reredos in three panels that takes up the whole back wall of the vast cell! And in the porch, as we enter this central chamber, how impressive are the carvings to right and left! On the left, in low relief, is a picture representing Shiva seated in meditation. The posture is that of Buddha, and it requires a few minutes of close examination to make sure of the distinction. The leopard-skin, the serpents, and the *jatil,*[1] however, are clear enough. There is no real ground for confusion. On our right is another low relief of Durga, throwing herself into the universe, in God intoxication. Behind her the very air is vocal with saints and angels chanting her praises. The whole is like a verse from *Chandi.* And we hold our breath in astonishment as we look and listen, for here is a freedom of treatment never surpassed in art, combined with a message like that of medieval Catholicism. The artist here uttered himself as securely as the Greek. It was only in the thing said that he was so different. And for a translation of that into terms European, it needs that we should grope our way back to Giotto and Fra Angelico and the early painters of missals.

Our astonishment is with us still as we penetrate the shadows and find our way amongst the grey stone pillars to that point from which we can best see the great central Trimurti of the reredos. How softly, how tenderly, it gleams out of the obscurity! Shadows wrought on shadows, silvergrey against the scarcely deeper darkness; this in truth is the very Immanence

1. Matted hair

of God in human life. On its right is the sculptured panel representing the universe according to the Shaivite idea. Shiva and Parvati ride together on the bull, and again as in the carving of Durga in the porch—the heavens behind them are like a chorus of song. On the left of the Trimurti, finally, is the portrayal of the world of the Vaishnavite. Vishnu the Preserver has for consort Lakshmi the Divine Grace and the whole universe seems to hail Him as God. It is the heads of Brahma, Shiva, and Vishnu, grouped together in one great image, that make up the Trimurti which fills the central recess between these panels.

A ledge for offerings runs along below this series of pictures. The altar itself, where actual consecration took place, is seen to the spectator's right, in the form of a little canopy-like shrine or Shiva chapel, which once doubtless held the four-headed Mahadeva that may today be seen outside the caves, and now contains the ordinary image of Shiva, as placed there at some later date. We may assume that lights and offerings, dedicated here, were afterwards carried in procession, and finally placed before the various divisions of the great reredos. The pillared hall held the congregation, and stands for the same thing as the nave in a Christian church, or the courtyard in a modern temple like Dakshineswar.

So much for the main cave. The plan of the entablature is carried out, however, in the architecture, and there are wings—consisting of cells built round courtyards enclosing tanks—to right and left of the great central chamber. And here the carved animals and other ornaments, that support short flights of stairs and terraces, are all eloquent of a great art period and a conception of life at once splendid and refined.

Elephanta, then, perpetuates the synthesis of Hinduism. How royal was the heart that could portray no part of his people's faith—even though it held his personal conviction and worship—without the whole! **Not Shaivite alone, but Shaivite, Vaishnavite, and the still remembered worshipper of Brahma, go to make up the Aryan congregation. All alike, it is felt, must be represented.** Nay, when we recall the older Kanheri, we feel that not the churches alone, but also the monastic orders outside all churches; not society only, but also the supersocial organisation, denying rank and all that distinguishes society, had a place here. In the architectural remains within a certain area of the Bay of Bombay, we have a perfect microcosm of the Indian thought and belief of a particular period. The question that presses for determination is, what was that period.

The first point to be noticed is the presence of Brahma in this synthesis of Hinduism. In the Mahabharata, similarly, we are constantly startled by the mention of Brahma. He is there called the Grandsire, the Creator, and sometimes the Ordainer, with face turned on every side. This last attribute is perhaps derived from some old mysticism, which gave the Romans Janus—from which our own January—and found expression amongst the Hindus in the four-headed image, and the weapon with four heads called Brahma's head, as mentioned in the Ramayana. While constantly referred to in the Mahabharata, however, Brahma is nowhere there invested with new functions. He does not appear as a growing concept of the divine.

He plays rather the part of one receding from actuality who must constantly be held in memory. In the Pauranika stories of Krishna, similarly, no one goes to Brahma with any prayer or austerity, as they do to Shiva.

He is no dynamic factor in the life of men. Yet He is the Creator, beyond all argument. He is chief and eldest of Hindu post-Vedic deities. His position needs no proving. It is accepted by all. Nor does Brahma in the Puranas require to be convinced that Vishnu is the equal of Himself: Krishna, as the presentment of Vishnu, is new to Him, but Vishnu himself He takes for granted. At the same time, while indisputably supreme, Brahma is by no means a spiritual reality. That place, as other stories and the whole of the Mahabharata show, is filled by Shiva, with whom are associated all those philosophical ideas nowadays described as Vedantic. And yet, if the story of Krishna had been written in the twentieth century, Brahma would have had no place in it at all. Partially forgotten as He was then, He is wholly forgotten now. From this evidence then, we may infer that the personality of Brahma was the first, and that of Shiva the next, to be developed as .concepts of Supreme Deity.

Thus there was a period in Hinduism when the name of Brahma, the Creator, was held in reverence—having dominated the theology of a preceding age—and used in conjunction with those of Shiva and Vishnu to make the specification of deity complete. **Hinduism at that time deliberately preached God as the Three-in-One, the Unity-in-Trinity. This theological idea we find expressed in its purity in the Caves of Elephanta,** and perhaps slightly later in the Ramayana of Valmiki.

The poet Kalidasa also, writing both the *Kumarasambhava* and the *Raghuvamsha,* would appear to have been under the inspiration of this Hindu idea of the Trinity. He shared the desire of the power that carved Elephanta to represent the synthesis of Hinduism by doing something to concretise both its popular aspects.

But the form under which Vishnu appears in Elephanta is purely theological. It is Lakshmi-Narayana, the idea that to this day is more familiar to the West and South of India than to Bengal. This. theological concept—or divine incarnation, as it is called—was fully formulated before the Ramayana was written, and is referred to there much oftener than in the Mahabharata; though that also was meant to prove the identity of a certain hero with Vishnu. Sita-Rama are from the very beginning argued as the bodying-forth of Lakshmi Narayana in human form. Krishna in the later epic seems to be consciously a second attempt to paint the mercy of God in incarnation.

The ideas that succeed in India are always firm-based on the national past. Thus that idealism of the motherland, which is today the growing force intellectually, can go back for foundation to the story of Uma, wedded in austerity to the Great God. Similarly, it would be very interesting to see worked out by some Indian scholar the root-sources in Vedic literature of these conceptions of Shiva and Vishnu. One can hardly resist the conclusion that each was elaborated independently in its own region.

We have to think of the Mother Church as the expression of a people who, between 500 B.C. and A.D. 500, were intensely modern and alive. Indian civilisation has educated its children from the beginning to the supreme function of realising ideas. And ideas grew and succeeded each other, taking on new forms with amazing rapidity, in the period immediately before and after the Christian era. The impression that the chief formative impulse here was the life and character of Buddha is extremely difficult to resist. On one side, the stern monastic; on the other, the very projection into humanity of the Infinite Compassion—the Blessed One was both of these. His character was the world's proof that God was at once Preserver of His children, and Destroyer of their Ignorance, even while He was but a name for the Supreme Itself. Hence in men's dreams of Shiva we see their effort thenceforth to realise the one, while Narayana is their personification of the other of these attributes.

Just as Buddha may have been the radiant centre whence diverged the popular religions, so **Banaras may have been the spot where the idea of Shiva was first conceived and elaborated.** Many causes may have contributed to this. The Deer Park, seven miles away, must have been a monastic university before the time of Buddha. Its undisputed pre-eminence is shown by the fact that He made His way to it immediately on attaining enlightenment, because it was there that His theory, or discovery, must be published to the world. From this we can see that the monk, although a little apart, must always have been an impressive figure in Banaras, which was itself, at this particular period, mainly a commercial and industrial centre, associated with a great Brahmanic wealth of Vedic memory.

After the time of Buddha, while his name still reverberated throughout the length and breadth of the land,

Banaras would doubtless become a place of pilgrimage, rendered doubly sacred by His memory and by its Vedic altar. **The growing opinion that the Deity could take no delight in slaughter must have killed the sacrifices, and the Brahmanas of Banaras would take to cherishing a system of theology in which the Great God was represented as remote, solitary, and meditative.** The right of all classes to interest themselves in religious philosophy was indisputable in face of the work done by the Buddhist Orders; and Vedantic theories and explanations were given freely to all comers, and by them carried back over the country to their distant homes.

We may suppose, meanwhile, that the memorial Stupas continued to be placed in the sacred city, as at other scenes of Buddhist memory, by pious pilgrims. Little by little the Stupas changed their shape. At first plain, or simply ornamented, they came to have the four Buddhas on them, looking North, South, East, and West. Some were then made, by a natural transition, with four large heads instead of four seated figures. According to the Brahmanas, the God of the Aryans was Brahma, the personal aspect of Brahman. According to the thought of the world at that period, again, God, or Brahma, was "the Ordainer, with face turned on every side." Hence the four-headed Stupa was first, perhaps, regarded as the image of Brahma. But it could not long be so taken. The new conception of God was growing, and **presently, with the post in the middle, it came to be regarded as Mahadeva, and then as Shiva.**

There was a good deal of hesitation at this period. Anyone who has seen the bathing ghat at Baragaon, between Bihar Sharif and Rajgir, will be in a position to judge in how many different directions the emblem of Shiva might have been evolved. The four-headed Stupa, for instance, was some- times made to refer to Parvati. Finally, however—with the perfecting of the theological idea of Maheshvara—the modified Stupa was taken as Shiva. This particular phase must have occurred just as the Rajputs began to settle in Rajputana, and this accounts for the prevalence of the four-headed Shiva in that country. The family-God of the royal line of Udaipur is said to be a four-headed Mahadeva. In Banaras again there may be more; but there is certainly one temple in the Tamil quarter behind the monastery of Kedar-Nath, where a Shiva of the period in question is worshipped to this day. When first erected, this temple was doubtless on a level with the street. Owing to the accumulation of debris in the interim, however, it is now some eight or ten steps down. This fact alone gives us some notion of the age of the building.

The image of Mahadeva has gone through many further phases of simplification since the day we speak of, but this Shiva of Banaras and the other of Elephanta belong to a single historic period, and the small four-headed Stupa outside the caves is one of their most precious relics.

Hinduism throbs with the geography and history of India. In every image of Shiva speaks the voice of pre-Gupta Banaras. In that complex conception of Krishna which blends in one the Holy Child of Vrindaban, the Hero of the Gita, and the Builder of Dwarka, we celebrate the vision of the royal house of Pataliputra. In the Ramayana we unravel the earlier dream of Kosala. And here in Elephanta on the extreme West, we are confronted with a rendering of the great synthesis that comes after the formulation of Shiva. Whence did Elephanta take her Lakshmi-Narayana? And what must have been the solidarity of the country when the dream dreamed in Banaras finds expression here a thousand miles away!

Wherever we turn, we are met by the same phenomenon of the marvellous and effective unity of pre-medieval India. There Narayana, who is constantly worshipped in Madras, is the same whose images were wrought in Bihar so long ago as the fifth century. A single style of architecture characterises a single period, from Bhubaneshwar to Chitor. Every child knows the names of the seven sacred rivers; and the perfect Tirtha, for every province of India, has taken a man these many centuries to the Himalayas, to Dwarka, to Cape Comorin, and to Puri.

•••

9

KRISHNA AND THE GOSPEL OF THE GITA

We worship Thee, seed of the universe,
Thou one unbroken Soul.
We worship Thee, whose footstool is worshipped by the gods.
Thou Lord of the saints,
Physician of the world-disease,
To Thy lotus-feet our salutation, O Great Soul!

Hindu form of salutation to a Divine Incarnation.

I

It is told of a certain Bodhisattva that, all his struggles done and illumination reached, he was about to pass over into Nirvana. But as his feet touched the threshold of supreme blessedness there rose to his ears the sound of the sorrowful crying of humanity. Then turned that great soul back from Nirvana and entered again into life, declaring that till the last grain of dust in the universe had passed in before him, he would by no means go into salvation. And this Bodhisattva is he who sits on the throne of the Dalai Lama in Tibet, watching the world of men with eyes of divine pity from afar off.

Called by various names, arrayed in widely differing garb, we come constantly in Hinduism on the attempt, as here in the story of the Dalai-Lama, to express the idea that in the great Heart of the Absolute there dwells an abiding charity towards men. It would seem as if, to the religious instinct of humanity, the dream of "the pursuit of the soul by God" is a necessity; and the Hindu, well aware of the impossibility of giving it logical expression, veils his effort in mythodology. Whence the stories of the Avatars. For our conception of the doctrine of reincarnation is only complete when we understand that now and again the Eternal Love is represented as projecting itself into the sphere of manifestation, taking shape as a man, in order to act as a lamp amidst the darkness of delusion, a counter-magnetism to the attractions of desire.

It is absurd, says the Hindu—whose imagination can never be charged with provincialism—to think that such an incarnation, supposing it to occur at all, could visit the world only once. Is respect of persons a divine attribute? Or is the need of mankind at any time less than complete? Can we believe, again, that the power of creative energy to assume and throw off the shell of personality is exhausted in a single effort? Rather must the taking upon Himself of mortal form and limitations be to the all-pervasive "as the lifting of a flower's fragrance by the summer breeze", a matter of play; or like the shining of a lamp through the window wherein it is set, without effort—nothing more.

The orthodox Hindu is thus usually in no position to deny the supernatural character of the Babe of Bethlehem. He is only unable to admit that the nature of Christ stands alone in the history of the world, holding that his own country has seen even more than the three—Rama, Krishna, and Buddha—who were His brothers. Still more cogently does he claim sometimes that all these and possibly others of whom he has not heard, are but one soul, one expression of Godhead coming back at different times to lay hold on the hearts of men. And he quotes in support of this contention the familiar words of Krishna: "Whenever religion decays, and when irreligion prevails, then I manifest myself. For the protection of the good, for the destruction of the evil, for the firm establishment of the Dharma, I am born again and again."

It is natural enough to the Hindu intellect that around each such forth-shining of the Divine should grow up a new religious system or church. But each of these is only a special way of expressing the one fundamental doctrine of Maya, a new mode of endearing God to man. At the same time it is thought that every one, while recognising this perfect sympathy of various faiths for one another, should know how to choose one amongst them for his own, and persist in it, till by its means he has reached a point where the formulae of sects are meaningless to him. "For it is good," say the people, "to be born in a church, though it is foolish to die there."

In this sense—somewhat different from the religious partisanship of Europe—the popular and growing belief of the Hindu masses consists of various forms of the worship of Krishna. It is this creed that carries to those who need it, a religious emotionalism like that of the Salvation Army or of Methodism. In the hottest nights, during periods of "revival", the streets of a city will be crowded with men bearing lights and banners, and dancing themselves into a frenzy to such words as:

Call on the Lord,
Call on the Lord,
Call on the Lord, little brother!
Than this name of the Lord,

For mortal man,
There is no other way.

Krishna, like Rama and like Buddha, is considered to be a special incarnation of Vishnu, God the Preserver. It is, therefore, pertinent to appeal to Him for the goods of life, for consolation in sorrow, for deliverance from fear. 'He is known as the Holy Child, born in humility amidst cowherds by the Jumna; the Gentle Shepherd of the People, the Wise Counsellor, the Blessed Lord, tender Lover and Saviour of the human soul; and by other names not less familiar to ourselves. It is an image of tbe Baby Krishna that the Indian mother adores as the Bambino, calling it "Gopala", her cowherd. His name fills gospels and poems, the folk-songs of all Hindu races are full of descriptions of Him as a cowherd wandering and sporting amongst His fellows; and childish literature is full of stories of Him, curiously like European tales of the Christ-child. To the ecstatic mystic, He is the Divine Spouse.

If we dip into His history we shall think it a strange medley. So many parts were never surely thrust upon a single figure ! But through it all we note the—predominant Indian characteristics—absolute detachment from personal ends, and a certain subtle and humorous insight into human nature.

His main spiritual significance for India does not, perhaps—with one exception—attach to that part of His life which is related in the Mahabharata, but rather to what is told of Him in the Puranas—works not unlike our apocryphal Gospels. But the one exception is important. It consists of no less an incident than that conversation with the cheftain Arjuna which comprises thekor Song of the Blessed One. Of this little poem—only some three or four times the length of the Sermon on the Mount, and shorter even than the Gospel of St. Mark—**it may be said at once that amongst the sacred writings of mankind there is probably no other which is at once so great, so complete, and so short. It provides the worship of Krishna—and incidentally all kindred systems—with that open door upon abstract philosophy without which no cult could last in India for a week. But it is by no means the property of the Vaishnavas exclusively. From Kashmir to Cape Comorin it is bone of the bone and. flesh of the flesh of all forms of religious thought.**

Its ideas are unmistakably Indian in colour: its feeling is just as unmistakably universal. The voice that speaks on the field of Kurukshetra is the same voice that reverberates through an English childhood from the shores of the Sea of Galilee. We read the gracious words: "Putting aside all doctrines, come thou to Me alone for shelter—I will liberate thee from all sins, do not thou grieve," "Fixing thy heart on Me, thou shalt, by My grace, cross over all difficulties", and we drop the book, lost in a dream of One who cried to the weary and heavy laden, "Come unto Me." We certainly now understand, and cannot again forget, that for the Indian reader the eyes of the Lord Krishna are most kind, His touch infinitely gentle, and His heart full of an exceeding great compassion, even as for us are the eyes and the hand and the heart of Him who spoke of Himself as the Good Shepherd.

Like our own Gospels, the Gita abounds in quaint and simple metaphors. "As a lamp in a sheltered spot, not flickering", must be the mind. All undertakings are surrounded with evil, "as fire with smoke". The round of worship is "as a wheel revolving". So great is wisdom that though thou shouldst be "even the most sinful of all sinners, thou shalt cross safely to the conquest of all sin by the bark of wisdom alone". One of the most beautiful, referring to those perceptions which constitute the Universe as we know it says, "All this is threaded upon Me as gems upon a string." Nothing is mentioned that would not be familiar to the poorest peasant, living on a fertile plain, diversified only by a river and an occasional walled city.

And indeed it was for these, labouring men, unlettered and poor, that the Gita, with its masterly simplicity, was written. To those who had thought salvation and the beatific vision as far beyond their attainment as a knowledge of the classics—to these humble souls the Divine Voice declares that, by worshipping God and doing at the same time the duty of his station, every man may attain perfection: "Better for one is one's own duty, however badly done, than the duty of another, though that be easy." Again and again, as we read the Gita, we are driven to the conclusion that we hear an infinite mercy addressing itself to a people who had imagined the knowledge of God to be the monopoly of priesthoods and religious orders, and bidding them be of good courage, for the true monk is he "who neither hates nor desires", the true worshipper anyone "who offers to Me with devotion even a leaf or a flower or a cup of water". No wonder that the Indian people, saluting a Divine Incarnation, call Him the physician of the world-disease! Never did speech know how to be more interior. "Those who worship Me, renouncing all actions in Me, regarding Me as supreme, meditating on Me with entire devotion, for them whose thought is fixed on Me, I become ere long, O son of Pritha; the Saviour out of the ocean of this mortal world." "For I am the abode of Brahman, the Immortal and the Immutable, the Eternal Substance, and the unfailing Bliss." We kneel in a vast silence and darkness, and hear words falling like water drop by drop.

Nothing is omitted from the Gita that the unconsoled heart requires. There are even the tender promises of daily bread, so dear to the anxious: "They who depend on Me, putting aside all care, whatsoever they need, I myself carry it to them," runs one verse. Of this a beautiful story is told in the villages. The Brahmin sat copying the text, but when the word "carry" had been written, he felt a doubt. "My dear," he said, turning to consult his wife, "thinkest thou not it is irreverent to say 'carry' here? Did not our Lord mean 'send'?" "Beyond a doubt, beloved," answered his wife, "it is as thou sayest. Let the word be 'send'." Then the man took his penknife and erased the word he had just written, substituting his own emendation for it. A moment later he rose up to go and bathe. But his wife stood before him with troubled face. "I told thee not," she said, "that there is no food in the house, and nought have I to cook for thee." The Brahmin smiled gently. "Let us call upon our Lord to fulfil His own promise," he replied quietly; "meantime, I shall go and bathe," and he passed into the next room. Only a few minutes had he gone, when his wife was called to the door by a beautiful youth, who stood there with a basketful of delicious foods, ready for eating. "Who sent me this?"

the woman asked in amazement. "Your husband called me to carry it," said the lad carelessly, putting the basket as he spoke into her hands. But to her horror, as he lifted his arms, the housewife noted cuts and gashes above his heart. "Alas, my poor child, who hath wounded thee?" she cried. "Your husband, mother, before he called me, cut me with a small sharp weapon," was the quiet answer. Dumb with astonishment, the Brahmin's wife turned away to bestow the viands he had brought, and when she came back to the door the youth had gone, At that instant her husband re-entered the room, having returned, as she supposed from bathing. Her wonder about the food was forgotten in indignant sympathy. "Why," she cried, "didst thou so hurt thy messenger?" The man looked at her without understanding. "Him whom thou sentest to me with food, as thou didst go to bathe," she explained. "To bathe !" he stammered, "I have not yet been !" Then the eyes of husband and wife met, and they knew both who had come to them, and how they had wounded the heart of the Lord. And the Brahmin returned to the sacred text, and once more erasing a word restored it to its original form, for there can be no doubt that the true reading is, "They who depend on Me, casting aside all care, whatsoever they need, I myself carry it to them."

Such are some of the associations which cling to the little image of Krishna that the children about Calcutta can buy for a few farthings. It is made of lime, and painted blue-for just as white, to the dweller amongst northern snows, signifies purity, so blue, the colour of sky and ocean, to the child of the South, is the token of the Infinite. The left hand of the image holds a flute to the lips; the right carries a thin golden scroll, referring to the Gita. The feet are crossed carelessly, like those of any strolling peasant-player, and the head is crowned. Simple toy as it is, there is hardly a detail of the composite figure in which a devotional system does not centre.

"O Thou that playest on the flute, standing by the water-ghats, on the road to Vrindaban!" sing the lovers of Krishna, and their hearts melt within them while they sing, pierced as by S. Teresa's wound of seraphic love. Of all its elements, however, there is none which has the unequalled importance to the world of the scroll in the right hand, both as throwing light on Indian habits of thought and as an exposition of the science of religion. The questions, therefore—On what fundamental experience does the Gita base itself? To what does it appeal? What does it single out in life as requiring explanation? What is its main imperative?—are of singular interest. **That place which the four Gospels hold to Christendom, the Gita holds to the world of Hinduism, and in a very real sense, to understand it is to understand India and the Indian people.**

II

It is believed by Hindus that when great forces are in action, on occasions such as those of battle and earthquake, a certain state of etheric vibration is produced, which makes it easy for minds trembling on the verge of supreme knowledge to vault the barricades of sense and find illumination. Perhaps this is because a great intensity of experience has to be found and transcended. Perhaps the conditions, apparently simple, are really more complex than this. At any rate, the story of the Bhagavad-Gita is of the coming of such beatitude to a young soldier named Arjuna some three thousand years ago.

Incidentally, the opening of the poem presents us with an impressive picture of an ancient battlefield. On the great plain of Kurukshetra, already the scene of the prayers and austerities of saints and pilgrims for hundreds of years, two armies face each other. The leaders of both sides occupy chariots drawn by white horses; over each waves his personal ensign; and each carries a conchshell, by way of trumpet, to enable him to give signals and enforce attention to his commands. Both armies are represented as great hosts, but indications are not wanting that that of Duryodhana, the usurper, under the leadership of Bhishma, is the larger and stronger. And this is natural, since Duryodhana, rightly or wrongly, is still suzerain of the whole country, while the five Pandava brothers, his cousins, are only bent on the recovery of their rights from him. We have to call to mind that this is an ancient battle, consisting of an immense number of small fights, before we are able to give our thoughts calmly to the narrative, for we are told that from all parts of the field and on both sides the white conchshells have been blown, giving the signal for assault, and that already "the discharge of weapons" has begun, when Arjuna requests Krishna, who is acting as his charioteer, to drive him into the space between the two hosts, that he may single out those with whom he is to enter into personal combat during the fray.

The sight of the foe, however, has an extraordinary effect on the mind of the chieftain. Instead of looking on his enemies with an accession of faith in the justice of his own cause and a heroic determination to struggle to the last in its defence, he seems to realise for the first time the consequences of the attack. Amongst the foe stand all he has ever loved or honoured—Bhishma, the head of his house, the adored grandsire of his childhood; Drona, to whom he owes his education, and for whom he cherishes a passionate reverence; and cousins and relatives innumer-able besides, of whom the very worst is an old playfellow or a gallant combatant in tourney. The path to victory lies through the burning-ghat of the dead! The ashes of all he loves are scattered there!

As he realises this, Arjuna's great bow slips from his hand, and he sinks to the floor of his chariot in despair. We must remember that this is no mere failure of courage. The soldier has been tried and proved too often to be open for a moment to such an imputation. Neither is he represented as entertaining the slightest doubt of ultimate triumph. To the fortunes of war he gives not a thought, assuming, as do all brave men, that they must follow the right. He simply realises that for the sake of a few years of dominion he is about, with his own hand, to rid the earth of everything he loves. He realises, too, that this widespread slaughter will constitute an enormous social disaster.

This feeling of Arjuna's finds religious expression: "I desire not victory, O Krishna, neither kingdom nor pleasures. ...It would be better for me if the sons of Dhritarashtra, arms in hand, should slay me, unarmed and unresisting, in the battle." Surely the moral situation is finely conceived! A prince, of the proudest lineage on earth, is eager to be offered up as a sacrifice rather than accept empire at the price to be paid for it. On the battlefield of life does any case need better stating? Yet this thirst for martyrdom, which looks so like renunciation, is really quite another thing. "Thou art grieved for those who require no grief, yet thou speakest words of wisdom," says Krishna. For, instead of the actual indifference to the world and to his own part in it, of one who perceives that all before him is unreal, Arjuna is betraying that determination to maintain things as they are which belongs to those who hold that affection at least is a very actual good. It is on this distinction that the whole treatise is based.

At first, indeed, the charioteer affects to meet the chieftain's hesitation with all the contempt of knighthood for panic. "Yield not to unmanliness, O son of Pritha!" he exclaims. "Ill doth it become thee. Cast off this base weakness, and arise, O terror of foes." It is not till Arjuna, with a touching acknowledgement of grief and confusion, makes a supreme appeal for intellectual enlightenment, that Krishna, in the character of divine teacher, enters on that immortal pronouncement regarding the real and unreal. which ends by sending the knight back to the duty of his birth, unshrinking, with the words: "Firm, with undoubting rnind, I obey Thy word."

As the dialogue proceeds, the dramatic element disappears. The echoes of battle die away. We are standing alone in some chamber of the soul, holding that colloquy between human and divine, finite and infinite, which never ceases during life for any one of us, however little able we may be to disentangle it from the voices of the world. At the culminating moment of the interview, when the worshipper receives the sudden revelation of all existing in and by the Lord Krishna, as mere multiform expression of His sole energy, even at this moment, and during the rapt and broken praise which follows it, we find nothing discordant in the *mise en scene*. A chariot of war has become, as only a Hindu pen could have made it, silent as any cell of meditation. The corner of a battlefield has grown as remote from the whirl of life as the inmost recesses of a heart at prayer.

The main argument is, as we might expect, that as all appearances are delusive, action is to the wise man indifferent, and should be performed, once he is sure that he is called to it, without fear of consequences. "Him the wise call a sage—the man whose undertakings are all devoid alike of objects and desires, whose acts have been burnt to ashes in the fire of wisdom." "Never did I not exist, nor thou, nor these rulers of men; and no one of us will ever hereafter cease to exist." Therefore, "Free from hope and from selfishness, without any anxiety of mind, plunge thou into battle!"

The words are addressed to one who is pre-eminently a man of action, a soldier—supposed, saving a due regard for his military honour! to be swayed by the passion for justice, and the impulse to defend it. These things being the stake, throw for them, and throw boldly, says Krishna, and as results, take whatever may chance to come. "Man has always the right to work: man has no right to the results of work," is as much the heart and core of the Gita, as "Thou hast no right to success if thou art not also equal to failure," is of Stoicism. In application the two doctrines seem identical, but we have only to read, in order to see the advantage which the idea of Maya gives to the Indain thinker. Clear, sharp, incisive as chisel-strokes, are the utterances of Epictetus: like thunderbolts out of a tropical night the words of Krishna.

The Gita, however, does not consist of a single chain of reasoning, moving in definite progression from beginning to end. Rather is the same thing said over and over again, in as many different ways as possible. Sometimes even a form of words is repeated, as if nothing mattered save to make the meaning clear. There is ample scope here for the digressive energy of ages, of which the outcome is the richly-woven texture, set here and there with those strangely cut Oriental jewels, which must remain amongst the greatest recorded words of religion to all time.

But readers will completely miss the sense of the Gita who permit themselves to forget its first ringing words: "Yield not to unmanliness, O son of Pritha! Ill doth it become thee. Shake off this base weakness, and arise, O terror of foes !". The book is nowhere a call to leave the world, but everywhere an interpretation of common life as the path to that which lies beyond. "Better for a man is his own duty, however badly done, than the duty of another, though that be easy." "Holding gain and loss as one, prepare for battle." That the man who throws away his weapons, and permits himself to be slain, unresisting, in the battle, is not the hero of religion, but a sluggard and a coward; that the true seer is he who carries his vision into action, regardless of the consequences to himself; this is the doctrine of the Gita, repeated again and again. The book is really a battle-cry. Spirituality is with it no retreat from men and things, but a burning fire of knowledge that destroys bondage, consumes sluggishness and egoism, and penetrates everywhere. Not the withdrawn, but the transfigured life, radiant with power and energy, triumphant in its selflessness, is religion.

The Gita is today the gospel of the Indian revival. And never was book so well suited to such function. For its eighteen chapters are the expression of an overwhelming national vitality. It is as true of peoples as of individuals, that when the age is full and rich, living is apt to outrun knowing. It is then that large questions press for solution. Great areas of experience require to be related to their common centre and to each other. And so pre-eminently does the Gita do this, that the Mussulman and the Christian can sit indifferently with the Hindu to gather its interpreta-tions.

The nature of all faith, the relation of all worship to worshipped and worshipper, the dependence of knowledge on non-attachment under all its forms: it is with problems like these, and not with any particular Credo, that the Gita concerns itself. It is at once, therefore, the smallest and most comprehensive of the scriptures of the world.

That indifference to results is the condition of efficient action is the first point in its philosophy. But there is no doubt that the action should be strenuous. Let every muscle be hard, every limb well-knit, let the mind sweep the whole horizon of fact; with the reins in hand, the fiery steeds under control, with the whole battlefield in view, and the will of the hero lifted high to strike for justice, "Arise!" thunders the voice of Shri Krishna, "and be thou an apparent cause!"

It is the supreme imperative. Play thy whole part in the drama of time, devoting every energy, concentrating the whole force. "As the ignorant act from selfish motives, so should the wise man act, unselfishly."

Just as the child sees the sun above his head, and the earth beneath his feet, distinguishing himself from both, while to the man of science, sun, planet, and child are all single points in a great ocean of force-matter, absolutely continuous from its centre to its farthest bounds, so to us all, in the sense-plane of thought, God, soul, and relation exist. Having reached that truth, however, which is the Beatific Vision, anyone of them will seem the whole, for all conception of limitation will be blotted out. As we ourselves are seen to be but light transformed; as thought and perception, life and motion, sun and planet, are all but different manifestations of a something that we call solar energy, so God, Self, and universe, are now known to be only distinctions made by sense in that one, Brahman, "the immortal and immutable, the eternal substance, and the unfailing Bliss."

An account of such a vision gives us the culminating chapter of the Gita. Krishna suddenly bursts forth on the sight of his astonished worshipper as the Universal Form, in Whom all that exists is one. Characteristically Indian in expression, full of the blaze and terror of the cosmos, this great scene can only perhaps be thoroughly appreciated by a Western mind if it has first understood something of the craving that it fulfils, caught some flash, may be, of the radiance it describes. Yet if the rest of the Gita were destroyed, this one chapter might take its place, for it makes all its logic actual. Arjuna's single sight becomes the sacrament of a whole world's hope.

It was midnight when I reached Thaneswar. The fierce white light of a tropical moon bathed the great common in front, where only trees and bushes, with their coal-black shadows, could be seen, and not a single human habitation was in sight. Behind, the dak-bungalow lay in darkness, and the train by which I had come had passed on long ago into the night. One was alone on the plain of Kurukshetra with. three thousand years.

But the silence did not remain unbroken. Clear and distinct on the still air rose the accents of the immortal dialogue. "Man has the right to work: man has no right to the fruits of work," said, once more, the Divine Charioteer. Yet many a memorable battle has been fought, India herself has heard a thousand dialogues, preaching the truths of the Bhagavad-Gita. Why, asked my heart, does one come to this spot? For what thing above all others, does the world remember Kurukshetra?

And then I saw why, never to forget. Kurukshetra was the place of the Great Vision, the field of the Divine Illumination of Arjuna.

●●●

10

THE STORY OF SHIVA

Thou that art knowledge itself,
Pure, free, ever the witness,
Beyond all thought and beyond all qualities,
To Thee, the only true Guru, my salutation,
Shiva Guru! Shiva Guru! Shiva Guru!

Salutation to Shiva, as the Teacher of the Soul.

In India's great moments, the Himalayas have always been her highway, not her boundary. Those strings of pack-mules, with their sorry-looking rice-bags, that we meet on every hill-path, as we wander through the mountains, are the remains of a great continental traffic that once carried the religion into China. For beliefs, like diseases, do not travel alone. The pilgrim is accompanied by the pedlar: the begging-friar dogs the footsteps of the merchant; the faith follows the line of trade. It may be that if Chinese silk and turquoise had not found their way to India many centuries before the birth of Buddha, the news of the Great Nirvana could never have reached the remoter East.

To this day, we find ancient capitals and their ruins, old fortresses, royal temples, scattered up and down the heights from Baluchisthan to Nepal, in regions long depopulated. And Himalayan shrines and cities have an art and architecture of their own, which is more severely beautiful, because more directly related to the common early Asiatic, than the later styles, to be found further south. For the first culture-area of humanity had these mountains as its rim. Long before a local prepossession had named the Mediterra-nean, Asia was. And of that Asia, Egypt, Greece, Etruria, were outlying provinces. The Saracen and Moor, with all that they brought of art and chivalry, with all the intellectual vividness they conferred on Europe, were but the relic-mongers of its past. In the West, even now, we admit a people to be civilised only if we can trace its intellectual descent from this ancient Asia.

Above all, it is the broken voices of its primitive consciousness that are hailed today in every civilised country as divine revelations. India herself is no exception to this rule. For all the migrations of Asokan and other periods pale beside the memory of the still more significant era when for the first time there came to settle on the Northern Plain those little communities of people, already agricultural and industrial in their habits, who carried with them the culture of Central Asia. It was not a regimented immigration. The Lall Kaffir, or pale folk, dwelling to this day in the Hindu Kush, were not deserters, turning aside from the line of march. We must rather suppose a gradual overflow, through many centuries, of the Himalayan region. And yet, at some time or place, it must have been sufficiently consolidated and self-organised to become conscious of its great heritage of thought, to commit its knowledge to writing, and to give form and definition to the Aryan civilisation.

Wherever and whenever it may have happened, this was the moment at which long ages of accumulating reflection and observation precipitated themselves into form as the Vedas. Even so are all scriptures born. The Tartar herdsman, facing his unknown future as a peasant, records at once his ideals and his memories, and we have the I-Ching or Book of Change, of the Chinese people. The austere self-isolation of a few tribes of Syrian shepherds fronts with terror the degradation of Babylonian cities, and the prophets pour out their sublime woes. The Latin Church carries to the Norse peasant with one hand the waters of baptism, with the other the script, by means of which he is to write down his magnificent sagas. The old order blossoms into complete self-consciousness at that very instant when every petal trembles to the fall.

So passed the Vedic age, for the Aryans settled down in India, and became Hindus. The process by which this was accomplished must have been complex and gradual. In some directions towards a greater luxury, it must have been fundamentally a simplification of life. The builders of the Himalayas had used wood and stone. The builders of the plains used bamboos, mud, and bricks; and their architectural designs began to approximate to those of pottery. The weavers of Central Asia had worked in wool, doubtless of marvellous dyes. The craftsmen of the South were driven to cotton and silk. That system of ritual purification which was common to the whole of the Asiatic culture, and which is still retained by Europe in the form of sacraments and rubrics, must have been deepened and extended to meet the new climatic conditions.

Natural metaphor underwent transformation. Coolness was exchanged for warmth as the qualification of friendship. Himalayan scenery was no longer present to give constant birth to grand myths and colossal imagery. That gradual absorption of regional thought and worship began, which was to produce what in its latest phase would be known as Hinduism. But it was always to be absorption. It was always to be the play of the Aryan intellect upon the indigenous symbol; never the acceptance of a superstition that could not be rationalised. This wonderful continuity of thinking marks the solidarity of Hinduism as nothing else could. Every creed within its frontiers—and they are wide enough to include all types of religious thought—can prove the Vedas to be its authority. Even the image of the Goddess Kali is held to be foreshadowed in the sublime Anthem to Creation of the Rig-Veda:

The Self sustained as cause below,
Projected as effect above.

We find in India, then, a classical nation like Egypt or Greece, which has been allowed to develop freely on the mental plane, and has held the thread of its thought unbroken to the present day. It may be said broadly that great culture and subjective philosophies are almost always continental in their origin, while the sense of nationality and insistence on the beautiful are insular. If this be true, it would explain the greater sympathy between Hellenic and Japanese developments than between Greek and Indian.

For the Hindu imagination long ago detached itself from the cycle of physical beauty, to seek its fullest satisfaction in subtler realms. This fact is extraordinarily evident in Kalidasa's poem of "The birth of the War-Lord", where he depicts the wooing of Mahadeva by Uma, the Himalayan princess. Here the poet places his heroine at the very acme of maidenly charm, kneeling in worship to lay flowers at the feet of the Great God, and having as her background the forest of plum and cherry and almond, all suddenly burst into blossom, because to them comes Spring, as the comrade of Love. And then, with a single sweep of the brush, the picture is blotted out: the Great God has vanished from beneath his cedar; Eros is burnt to ashes; and the royal maiden kneels alone, while the bitter wailing of Desire, the beautiful wife of Love, fills the whole woodland. Uma's triumph is reached, and the Divine Spouse drawn to her side, only when, in the midst of unheard of austerities, she gives supreme proof of courage and devotion as nun and worshipper instead of woman and lover. This touch lies far beyond the range of the Greek.

A similar tendency to use physical symbolism as a system of notation merely, instead of seeking in it the direct and adequate expression of spiritual conceptions, as did the classical genius of Europe, is to be found throughout the whole conception of Shiva or Mahadeva, the Great God Himself. The tiger-skin in which he is clad, and some of the names of this deity, induce Tod in his "Annals of Rajasthan" to regard Him as simply a new version of the Greek Bacchus. It is a great deal more likely that behind the two, in the dim North, and in the distant past—in some Lake Manasarovar of thought, to quote Max Muller—there may loom up a common ancestor. But this probability only makes more significant the divergences between the two conceptions.

Anyone who visits Northern India must desire to know the meaning of the little black stones under every conspicuous tree, which are so evidently set up for worship. They are said by Europeans to be of phallic origin; but if so, Hindus are no more conscious of the fact than we are of the similar origin of the maypole. Wherever one goes, one finds them, by the road-sides in cities and villages, on the river-banks, or inside the entrance to a garden, if there is a tree that stands alone. For in such places one is glad to think that the Great God, begging His handful of rice from door to door, may have seated Himself to bless us with His meditation.

The small stone pillar, called the Linga—the word Lingam is literally symbol—may have been taken from the bed of a stream, and in that case is likely to be of a long egg-shape. But if it has been cut by the hand of man, it is short and slightly tapering, with a thimble-like top. Sometimes, in all good faith, the features of a human face have been more or less crudely marked on it, with white paint. In any case, it is only a question of time till some woman, passing by on her way from bathing, stops to pour a little water, or sprinkle a few grains of rice tenderly over the head of the stone, perhaps also to add bael-leaves, trifoliate like our clover; or a garland of white flowers; or, prompted by a heart more devoted and loving than usual, to touch it with a spot of sandal-paste, so cool and refreshing in this hot climate! Then the earth is touched with the head, and the worshipper passes on.

The simple act is not without its perplexities, and we seek for interpretation. At first in vain. Or the explanations given are more bewildering than helpful. Hindus are too conscious of the symbolistic nature of every faith, and too sensitive also to the scornful irreverence of most foreign inquirers, to speak out, or argue out, the heart of their heart with the passing stranger. Rather they will turn on one, with a strange pity. "Do you not understand," they will say, "that this is the Great God who is emblemed here?" He can have neither visitor, nor history, nor worshipper. Such things are vain dreams of men. Only for our own hearts' ease, and to carry ourselves nearer to the inner vision, do we set up a stone whereon we may offer rice and water and lay a leaf or two !" It will be difficult in all India to find a woman so simple, or a peasant so ignorant, that to them worship is not, as some one has said, "a conscious symbolism, instead of a fragment of primitive personification". Yet by degrees the great myth leaks out. Little by little we learn the associations of the name.

Linga, after all, is but a fragment of stone. Far better images of Mahadeva are those who come and go yonder, amidst the passing crowd—the monks and beggars, some clad only in ashes with matted hair, others with shaven head, and clothed from throat to foot in the sacred yellow, but most of them bearing one form or another of staff or trident, and carrying a begging bowl. And finer still will these be, when, retiring into the forest, or climbing to the verge of eternal snows, they sit, even like this stone Linga, bolt upright in the shelter of tree or rock, lost to the world without, in solitary meditation.

About the whole conception there is a striking reminiscence of the Himalayas. Whether we will or not we are carried back, as we listen, to the great age of the Vedas, when the Aryan immigration was still taking place. It is a day of sacrifice, and at the forest-clearing people and priests are met, to heap the offerings on the mighty fire, chanting appropriate texts. Hour after hour, sometimes day after day, the mound of pure flame lasts; and long after it has ceased the hot white ashes lie in their immense bed, thrilling now and then to a faint trickling spark, sighing themselves out into the coldness of death. Who was it that first came and rubbed himself with those soft white ashes, in order to be clothed upon with the worship of God and separation from the world? Who was it that first retired into cave or jungle, and meditated, until his hair became a tangled mass, and his nails grew long, and his body emaciated, and he still pursued the sublime bliss of the soul? However the idea of such an exterior grew, the whole genius of India has spoken for many a century in just such a picture—the hermit clad in wood-ashes, with masses of neglected hair, piled on the top of his head, indifferent to the whole world, bent only on thought.

As the Aryans wandered in sight of the snow-mountains, with the fire-sacrifice for their central rite, an indissoluble connection arose in their minds between the two ideas. Were not the flames of the offerings white like the Himalayas, always mounting upward like the aspiring peaks, leaving behind them ashes for eternal frost. Those snowy heights, we must suppose, became the central objects of their love. Lifted above the world in silence, terrible in their cold and their distance, yet beautiful beyond all words, what are they like? Why, they are like—a great monk, clothed in ashes, lost in his meditation, silent and alone! They are like—like—the Great God Himself, Shiva, Mahadeva!

Having arrived at this thought, the Hindu mind began to work out all sorts of accessories and symbols, in which sometimes the idea of flame, sometimes of mountain, sometimes of hermit is uppermost—all contributing to the completed picture of Shiva, the Great God.

The wood was borne to the sacrifice on a bull: Shiva possesses an old bull, on which he rides. As the moon shines above the mountains, so He bears on His forehead the new moon.

Like the true ascetic, begging food at the householder's door, He is pleased with very simple gifts. The cold water of the bath, a few grains of rice, and two or three green bael-leaves, are His whole offering in the daily worship. But the rice and water must be of the purest, for they are presented to a most honoured guest. Evidently the bael-leaf, like the shamrock, refers to the Trinity. For, as we all know, this doctrine is. Hindu as well as Christian and Egyptian.

To show how easily Shiva can be pleased, the people tell a pretty story. A poor huntsman—that is to say, one of the lowest of the low—once came to the end of a day's hunting without having snared or killed a single creature. Night came on, and he was far from home, in the jungle, alone. Near by stood a bael-tree, with branches near the ground, and he was glad to climb into it, to pass the night in shelter from wild beasts.

But as he lay crouching in its branches, the thought of his wife and children starving at home would come to him, and for pity of their need great tears rolled down his cheeks, and falling on the bael-leaves broke them by their weight, and carried them to the ground. Under the sacred tree, however, stood a Shiva-Linga, image of Shiva, and the tears fell, with the leaves, on its head. The night a black snake crept up the tree, and stung the man. Arid bright spirits came, and carried his soul to Heaven, and laid it down at the feet of Shiva.

Then, in that holy place, rose the clamour of many voices questioning: "Why is this savage here? Has he not eaten impure foods? Has he offered right sacrifices? Has he known the law?" But the Great God turned on them all in gentle surprise: "Did he not worship Me with bael-leaves and with tears?" He said.

Looking closer at the flame, however, one thing was very clear. It was white, but it had a blue throat—we see it even when we light a match!—and in order to bestow a blue throat upon Shiva, the following story arose:

Once upon a time, all the splendour and glory of the gods seemed to be vanishing from them. (Are such tales, we wonder, a reminiscence of the period when the old gods, Indra, Agni, and the lords of the universe, found themselves growing unfashionable, because the Trinity, Brahma-Vishnu-Shiva, was coming into favour?) What to do, the gods did not know, but they determined to pray to Vishnu, the Preserver of the World, for advice. He told them, perhaps contemptuously, to "go and churn the ocean" and the poor gods trooped forth eagerly to do His bidding.

They churned and churned. Many great and splendid things came foaming up and they seized them with avidity, here a wonderful elephant, there a princely horse, again a beautiful wife for some one. Each was only greedy to be first in the handling of the next delight, when all at once something black began to come. Welling up and up, and then spreading over the whole ocean, it came. "What is it?" they asked each other in horror. It was poison—death to them, death to the world, death to the universe. It came to their very feet, and they had to retreat rapidly in fear. Already they were in the midst of darkness, and there was nowhere that they could flee, for this dense blackness was about to cover all the worlds. In this moment of mortal terror, all the gods with one voice called on Shiva. He had taken no part in the receiving of gifts, maybe He would be able to help them now. Instantly, the great White God was in their midst. He smiled gently at their dilemma and their fear, and stooping down He put His hand into the waves, and bade the poison flow into the hollow of His palm. Then He drank it, willing to die, in order to save the world. But that which would have been enough to destroy all created beings was only enough to stain His throat, hence He bears there a patch of blue for ever.

Perhaps one of the most characteristic myths that have clustered round the name of Mahadeva is the Legend of the Boar-Hunt. As we read it, we stand on the snowy heights of the third range of the Himalayas, and seem to watch a mighty snow-storm sweeping through the ravine before us.

Arjuna, one of the principal heroes of the Great War, and the second figure in the dialogue of the Gita, had gone up into the mountains, to spend three months in worshipping Shiva, and invoking His blessing. Suddenly one day as he was praying and offering flowers before the Linga, he was roused by a wild boar, which was rushing forward to attack him. It was only an instant, and Arjuna, the practised archer, had seizd his bow and shot the animal. But at the selfsame moment a shout of warning was heard, and simultaneously with Arjuna's second arrow pierced the body of the beast. The hero raised his eyes, and saw, coming towards him, a formidable-looking hunter and huntress, followed by an innumerable retinue of women, attired for the chase, and attended, at some distance, by a dim host of shadows—the armies of demons and hobgoblins. A second later, the whole hunt had come to a stop before him.

"The quarry was mine!" cried the Hunter—and his voice sounded like the winter-blasts, amongst the mountains—"the quarry was mine. Mine is the lordship of these forests! How dared you touch it?"

At this address, Arjuna blazed with anger, and picking up the bow and arrows that he had thrown aside before returning to his worship, he challenged the Hunter to a personal combat.

"Accepted," was the reply, and the duel began. But to the hero's dismay, he seemed to be attacking some terrible phantom, for, one after another, his good stout arrows disappeared into the person of his antagonist, working him no harm.

"Let's wrestle then!" shouted Arjuna, and casting aside his bow, he flung himself upon his foe. He was met by the quiet touch of a hand on his heart, and fell to the ground stunned.

"Well, come on!" said the Hunter, as he recovered himself a few seconds later, and turned aside from the contest. But he seemed almost intoxicated. "I must finish my worship first," he said, in a thick voice, taking up a garland of flowers, to fling about the Shiva-Linga. The next moment the eyes of Arjuna were opened, for the Hunter towered above him, blessing him, and the flowers were about his neck.

"Mahadeva! Mahadeva!" cried the worshipper, flinging himself on the ground, to touch with his head the feet of the God. But already the hunt had swept on down the valley, and the Hunter and Huntress had disappeared, with all their train.

Such are a few of the stories told of Shiva, so deeply loved by all his devotees. To them there is nothing in the world so strong and pure and all—merciful as their great God, and the books and poems of Hindus are very few in which he is not referred to with this passionate worship.

Sometimes He is entirely a personification of the Himalayas, as when the Milky Way is made to fall upon his head, wander round and round amongst the tangled locks, and issue from them at last as the Ganges. Indeed, the imagination of the people may be said to make of their northern ranges one vast shrine to Him; for it is far away, they say, across the frost-bound heights, where the Himalayas are at their mightiest and India passes into Tibet, that the Lake Manasarovar lies, at the foot of the great ice-peak of Kailas. Here is the reign of silence and eternal snow, and here, guarding the north, is the holy home that Shiva loves.

He is the very soul of gentleness, refusing none. Up here have gathered round Him all those who were weary of earth, having found no acceptance amongst the fortunate. The serpents, whom all the world hates and denies, come to Kailas, and Mahadeva finds room for them in His great heart. And the tired beasts come—for He is the refuge of animals—and it is one of these, a shabby old bull, that He specially loves and rides upon.

And here, too, come the spirits of all those men and women who are turbulent and troublesome and queer, the bad boys and girls of the grown-up world, as it were. All the people who are so ugly that no one wants to see them; those who do things clumsily, and talk loudly, and upset everything, though they mean no harm, and the poor things who are ridden by one idea, so that they never can see straight, but always seem a little mad—such are the souls on whom He alone has mercy. He is surrounded by them, and they love and worship Him. He uses them to do His errands, and they are known as Shiva's demons.

But Shiva is more even than this. He is the Self-born, the eternally-existent postulate of freedom and purity and light. He is the great teaching soul of things. His function is to destroy ignorance, and wherever knowledge is achieved, He is, His name of "Hara! Hara!" ("The Free! The Free!") was the battle-cry of the Mahrattas. More yet, He is Rudra, the Storm, the Terrible; and it is under this aspect that Hinduism raises to Him its daily cry:

Evermore protect us—O thou terrible!—
From ignorance, by thy sweet compassionate face.

For, after all, a human quality is always limited to one of two, the Divine must be lifted above good as well as evil, above joy as well as pain. We have here the Indian conception of same-sightedness, and perhaps its devotional significance is nowhere interpreted as in the Hindi song of Surdas, which is here repeated as a nautCh-girl was heard to sing it in a Rajput Court:

O Lord, look not upon my evit qualities!
Thy name, O Lord, is Same-sightedness,
By Thy touch, if Thou wilt, Thou canst make me pure.[1]

One drop of water is in the sacred Jumna,
Another is foul in the ditch by the road-side,
But when they fall into the Ganges,
Both alike become holy.

One piece of iron is the image in the temple,
Another is the knife in the hand of the butcher,
But when they touch the philosopher's stone,
Both alike turn to gold.

So, Lord, look not upon my evil qualities!
Thy name, O Lord, is Same-sightedness,
Make us both the same Brahman.

•••

1. Literally, Make us both the same Brahman—i.e., let the Singer—low dancing-girl as she may be—become one with God Himself in the Supreme Essence, Brahman.

11

THE CITIES OF BUDDHISM

From Patna on the east to Banaras on the west, stretch in the month of January fields of white poppies all abloom. In this Holy Land of the Buddhist nations blossoms today this flower of death. The earth where it grows was made sacred long ago by the feet of Buddha. At the site of the ancient Pataliputra, almost where Bankipore stands today, He entered the kingdom of Magadha. For ages they called the river-crossing Gautama's Ferry, and told how on his last journey north He stood and watched the building of the first of its fortifications, foretelling the future greatness of the capital.

In remote villages one constantly comes upon images of Buddha, worshipped inside or outside the temples of Brahmana priests. In any field the peasant ploughing may turn up a relic or a fragment of carved stone. And under trees and bushes along the high-road one notes that three little heaps of mud standing side by side, that indicate a shrine of Jagannatha the Lord of the Universe, name and symbol of Buddha himself. They have forgotten Him maybe, yet remember His memory, these simple worshippers of the Bihari villages. To far distant lands, and to scriptures written in a long forgotten tongue, the modern organisation of scholarship has to go, to bring back to them the knowledge of Him whom under obscure names they worship to this day, in the very countryside where He lived and taught. A vague tradition of infinite mercy is all that remains amongst the unlearned of that wondrous personality. But this, after two thousand years, they cherish still. He belongs in a special degree to this peasantry of Magadha. There runs in their veins the blood of those whom He patted on the head as children. He taught them the dignity of man. He called upon them, as upon the proudest of his peers, to renounce and find peace in the annihilation of Self. To Gautama Buddha the peasant of Bihar owes his place in Hinduism. By Him he was nationalised.

Even in those stories of Buddha which remain to us it is explicitly stated that He sought amongst all existing solutions for the truth. This is the meaning of his travelling with the five ascetics and torturing the body with fasts. The first effort of a new thinker must always be to recapitulate existing systems and sound them to their depths. The Prince Gautama in the year 590 B.C. in the populous districts of the Sakya kingdom, awakening suddenly to the sense of his own infinite compassion, and to the career of a world-thinker, feels an overpowering need to meet with the scholars of his age, and makes his way, therefore, towards the neighbourhood of Rajgir in the kingdom of Magadha. From purely geographical considerations, we can see that there was doubtless another culture-centre, even so early as the age in question, at Taxila, in the extreme north-west. Indeed, towards the end of the life of Buddha himself, we are told of a lad who went there from Magadha—as European students of the Middle Ages to Cordova—to study medicine.

It is also easy to infer that the learning which could be acquired at Taxila was somewhat cosmopolitan in its character. The knowledge of herbs is a comparative science, and Taxila was on the high-road to Persepolis and Babylon, as well as to China and Nineveh. It was the doorway of India, or at least the university which had grown up beside that doorway; and that it was known as such among other nations is shown by the fact that Alexander came that way in 326 B.C. For the purchase of foreign stuffs, for knowledge of the geography that lay beyond her own border, for foreign news and foreign learning, possibly even for secular science as a whole, India had no centre like Taxila.

It follows with equal clearness that for the headquarters of a strictly national culture one would look nearer to the valley of the Ganges. Even the least organised of systems will somewhere have its central ganglion; and the fact that the Indian ganglion lay two centuries later in Magadha, is proved by the retirement of Chandra Gupta to Pataliputra after his defeat of the Greeks.

It was evidently not absurd with the means then at the disposal of the crown to look from that distance to mobilise armies on the frontier. But if military plans could be carried out so far from their base as this, then we cannot object that Magadha was too remote to be the religious centre of the whole. Banaras and Baidyanath are still left at its two extremes to tell us of the spiritual energy of its great period. The miracle that puzzles the imagination of historians—the sudden inception in the sixth century B.C. of religions of conscience in place of religions of power—is, rightly viewed, no miracle at all. These religions themselves were always there; it was only their organisation that began with the date named.

The events of history follow sequences as rigid as the laws of physics. **Buddha was the first of the faith-organisers, and first in India of nation-builders. But Buddha could not rise and do his work until the atmosphere about him had reached a certain saturation-point in respect to those ideas which the Upanishads preach.** The founders of religions never create the ideas they enforce. With deep insight they measure their relative values, they enumerate and regiment them; and by the supreme appeal of their own personality they give them a force and vitality unsuspected. But the ideas themselves were already latent in the minds of their audience. Had it not been so, the preacher would have gone uncomprehended. Through how many centuries had this process of democratising the culture of the Upanishads gone on? Only by flashes and side-gleams, as it were, can we gather even the faintest idea.

It is partly the good and partly the bad fortune of Buddhistic movements in India that, from their association with an overwhelming individualised religious idea, they appear to us as a sudden invention of the human mind in such and such a year. We do not sufficiently realise that they, together with all the words and symbols associated with them, must have been taken from a pre-existent stock of customs and expressions already long familiar to the people amongst whom Buddhism grew up. We imagine the great Chandra Gupta to have been the first monarch in India of an organised empire, but the words of Buddha himself, "They build the Stupa over a Chakravarti Raja—a suzerain monarch—at a place where four roads meet," show that the people of that early period were familiar enough with the drama of the rise and fall of empires, and that the miracle of Chandra Gupta's retirement to Pataliputra, thence to rule as far as the Punjab and the Indian Ocean, was in fact no miracle at all, since the India of his time was long used to the centralised organisation of roads, diks, and supplies, and to the maintenance of order and discipline.

The peculiar significance of Bihar in the comity of the Indian peoples rises out of its position on the frontier-line between two opposing spiritual influences. To this day it is the meeting place of Hinduistic and Mussulman civilisations. Sikh and Arya Samaji and Hindusthani Rajput pour down the waterway of the Ganga, to go no farther east than the twin-cities of Patna and Bankipore, and these stand face to face with the unified and Sanskritic civilisation of Lower Bengal. All sorts of modified institutions, representing mutual assimilation, arise along the border-line. Costume, language, manners, and habits of life are all full of this compromise. The old standard of culture, which even yet is not wholly dead, along a line stretching from Patna through Banaras to Lucknow, required of the highest classes of Hindus the study of Persian as well as Sanskrit, and one of the most liberal and courtly types of gentlehood that the world has seen was moulded thus.

The fertile country of Bengal, closely settled and cultivated, organised round the monarchy of Gour, and claiming a definite relation to Banaras and Kanauj as the sources of its culture, cannot, at any time within the historical period, have been susceptible of chaotic invasion or colonisation. The drift of unorganised races could never pass through Bihar, which must always have been and remains to the present the most cosmopolitan province of India. It has doubtless been this close contiguity of highly-diversified elements within her boundaries that has so often made Bihar the birth-place of towering political geniuses. The great Chandra Gupta, his grandson Asoka, the whole of the Gupta dynasty, Sher Shah, and finally Guru Govind Singh, are more than a fair share of the critical personalities of Indian history for one comparatively small district to have produced. Each of the great Biharis has been an organiser. Not one has been a blind force, or the tool of others. Each has consciously surveyed and comprehended contemporary conditions, and known how to unify them in himself, and to give them a final irresistible impulsion in a true direction.

Accepting the theory that Buddhism was developed in India, not as a sect or church, but only as a religious order, founded by one of the greatest of the World-Teachers, we find ourselves compelled to account for the relations that would arise between the king or the populace impressed by the memory of Buddha, and the order that followed in his succession and bore his name.

To do this, however, it is first necessary that we should have some determinate idea as to where, in the India of the Buddhist period, were the great centres of population. An Indian city, it has been well said, is a perishable thing, and it is easy to think of names which would justify the statement. No one who has seen the

Dhauli Rock, for instance, seven miles away from Bhubaneshwar, can imagine that the edict it bears, fronted by the royal cognisance of the elephant- head, was originally sculptured in the wild woods where it now stands. A glance is enough to tell us that the circular ditch which surrounds the fields below was once the moat of a city, backed and fortified by the Dhauli Hill itself, and that the edict-bearing rock stood at the south-eastern corner of this city, where the high-road from the coast must have reached and entered the gates.

The city of Dhauli was the capital, doubtless of Kalinga, when Asoka, in his military youth, conquered the province. In order to estimate its value and importance in the age to which it belonged, we must first restore to the mind's eye the ports of Tamralipti and Puri, deciding which of these two was the Liverpool of the Asokan era. A theocratic institution such as pilgrimage is frequently a sort of precipitate from an old political condition, and almost always embodies elements of one sort or another which have grown up in a preceding age. Presumably, therefore, Puri was the great maritime centre of the pre-Christian centuries in Northern India; and if so a road must have passed from it; through Dhauli, to Pataliputra in the north. By this road went and came the foreign trade between India and the East, and between the north and south.

In the age of the Keshari kings of Orissa, not only had Dhauli itself given place to Bhubaneshwar, but Puri, perhaps by the same process had been superseded by Tamralipti, the present Tamluk. It was at the second of these that Fa Hian in the fifth century embarked on his return voyage. Such a supersession of one port by another, however, would only be completed very gradually; and for it to happen at all, we should imagine that there must have been a road from one to the other along the coast. If only the covering sands could now be excavated along that line, there is no saying what discoveries might be made of buried temples and transitional cities. For a whole millennium in history would thus be brought to light.

On the great road from Dhauli to the north, again, there must have been some point at which a route branched off for Benaras, passing through Gaya, and crossing the Punpun River, following in great part the same line by which Sher Shah's dak went later and the railway goes today.

Let us suppose, however, that two thousand and more years have rolled away, and that we are back once more in that era in which Dhauli was a fortified capital city. The elephant-heralded decree stands outside the gates, proclaiming in freshly-cut letters of the common tongue the name of that wise and just Emperor who binds himself and his people by a single body of law.

"I, King Piyadassi, in the twelfth year after my anointing, have obtained true enlightenment," the august edict begins. It goes on to express the royal distress at the imperialistic conquest of the province, in Asoka's youth, and assures his people of his desire to mitigate this fundamental injustice of his rule by a readiness of give audience to any one of them, high or low, at any hour of the day or night. It further enumerates certain of the departments of public works which have been established by the new government, such as those of wells, roads, trees, and medicine. And it notes the appointment of public censors or guardians of morality.

In his reference to the obtaining of "true enlightenment" Asoka records himself a non-monastic disciple of the great monastic order of the day. Nearly three hundred years have elapsed since the passing of the Blessed One, and in the history of the Begging Friars whom he inaugurated there has been heretofore no event like this, of the receiving of the imperial penitent into the lay-ranks served by them. Their task of nation-making is slowly but surely going forward nevertheless. In the light of the Gospel of Nirvana the Aryan Faith is steadily defining and consolidating itself. The Vedic gods have dropped out of common reference. The religious ideas of the Upanishads are being democratised by the very labours of the Begging Friars in spreading those of Buddha, and are coming to be regarded popularly as a recognised body of doctrine charaacteristic of the Aryan folk. Vague racial superstitions about snakes and trees and sacred springs are tending more and more to be intellectually organised and regimented round the central figure of Brahma, the creator and ordainer of Brahmanic thinkers.

Thus the higher philosophical conceptions of the higher race are being asserted as the outstanding peaks and summits of the Hinduistic faith, and the current notions of the populace are finding their place gradually in the body of that faith, coming by degrees into organic continuity with the lofty abstractions of the Upanishads. In other words, the making if Hinduism has begun.

The whole is fermented and energised by the memory of the Great Life, ended only three centuries agone, of which the yellow-clad brethren are earnest and token. Had Buddha founded a church, recognising social rites, receiving the new-born, solemnising marriage, and giving benediction to the passing soul, his personal teachings would have formed to this hour a distinguishable half antagonistic strain in the organ-music of Hinduism. But he founded only an order. And its only function was to preach the Gospel and give individual souls the message of Nirvana. For marriage and blessing, men must go to the Brahmanas: the sons of Buddha could not be maintainers of the social polity, since in his eyes it had been the social nexus itself which had constituted that World, that Maya from which it was the mission of the Truth to set men free.

The work of the monk, then as a witness to the eternal verities, was in no rivalry to the more civic function of the Brahmanic priesthood. And this is the fact which finds expression in the relation of the monkhood to the Indian' cities of the Asokan era. The Brahmana is a citizen-priest, living in a city. The Buddhist is a monk, living in an abbey. In all lands the monk has memorialsed himself by buildings instead of by posterity. In India these have been largely carved, as at Mahaballipuram in the south, or excavated, as at Ellora and elsewhere, instead of built. But the sentiment is the same. **In place of a single monastery with its chapel or cathedral, we find here a number of independent cells or group of cells, and frequently a whole series of cathedral shrines. Apparently a given spot has remained a monastic centre during generation after generation.** Dynasties and revolutions might come and go but this would remain, untouched by any circumstances save the inevitable shifting of population and the final decay of its own spiritual fire.

In its decoration the abbey would reflect the art of the current epoch. In culture it would act as a university. In ideals it represented the supersocial, or extra-civic conception of the spiritual equality and fraternity of all men. Its inmates were vowed to religious celibacy. And we may take it that the place of the abbey would always be at a certain distance from a city whose government was in sympathy with it.

Thus the city of Dhauli, under the Emperor Asoka and succeeding worshippers of Buddha, had Khandagiri at seven miles distance as its royal abbey. The civic power was represented at Gaya: the monastic at Bodh-Gaya. Banaras was the seat of Brahmanas, Sarnath of monks. Elephanta was the cathedral-temple of a kings capital, but Kanheri, on another island a few miles away. offers to us the corresponding monastery.

From these examples and from what we can see to have been their inevitableness, we might expect that any important city of the Buddhistic period would be likely to occur in connection with a monastic centre some few miles distant. Now it is possible to determine the positions of a great many such cities on grounds entirely a priori. It is dear, for instance, that whatever geographical considerations might make Banaras great would also act at the same time to distinguish Allahabad. By a similar induction, Mathura on the Jamuna and Hardwar on the Ganges might also be expected to furnish proof of ancient greatness. Now outside Prayag we have to the present time, as a haunt of Sadhus, the spot known as Nirvanikal. And in the vicinity of Hardwar is there not Hrishikesh? The caves of Ellora have near them the town of Roza. But this we must regard as a sort of Mohammedan priory, inasmuch as its population consists mainly of religious beggars (of course not celibate) living about the tomb of Aurangzeb. The neighbouring capital that supported the youth of Ellora was probably at Deogiri, now called Daulatabad.

It is the broken links in the chain, however, that fascinate us most in the light of this historical generalisation. What was the city, and what the state, that made Ajanta possible? What was the city that corresponded to the Dharmashala at Sanchi? What was the city, and what the abbey, in the case of Amaravati?

Undoubtedly a fashion once started in such strength under Buddha-worshipping sovereigns and common wealths would tend to be imitated in later ages when the system of ideas that we know as Hinduism had come more definitely into vogue. It is also possible that when the Buddhistic orders failed or died out, their places were sometimes taken, in the ancient Maths and foundations, by Jain religious. Something of this sort appears at least to have happened at Sarnath and possibly at Khandagiri also. But the whole history of the relations between Brahmanas, Buddhists, and Jains wants working out from an Asiatic and not European point of view, if many pages of history are to become clear to us.

One question of great interest that arises in this connection is: What of this parallelism in the case of Pataliputra? Going back to Rajgir, we see the early ancestral capital of the Nanda kings confronted, at least in later ages, by Nalanda, the historic university of Bengal, to which Hiuen Tsang owed so much. But what of Pataliputra itself? Can we suppose that the imperial seat had no official Ashrama of piety and learning in its vicinity? Yet if it had, and if perhaps the "Five Pahars" mark the site of this religious college, what was the situation of the capital in regard to it?

Again we find place and occasion, by means of this generalisation, for more definite consideration than was hitherto possible of Indian culture and civilisation at various epochs. What were the various functions performed by these great extracivic priories? No Englishman has reason to be prouder of Oxford than the Hindu of Ajanta. The eternal antithesis of Europe between "town and gown" was never a source of rioting and disorder in the East, only because from the beginning they were recognised by universal consent as distinct entities, whose separateness of interests demanded a certain geographical distance. What was the life lived in these royal abbeys, whose foundations date back in so many cases—notably Bodh-Gaya, Sarnath, Dhauli, and Sanchi—even earlier than the reign of Asoka himself? They were a symbol of democracy to the eyes of the whole community, of the right of every man to the highest spiritual career. It is not conceivable that they should have been entirely without influence on the education of youth. But undoubtedly their main value intellectually lay in their character of what we should now call postgraduate universities.

Here must have been carried on such researches as were recorded, in the lapse of centuries, by Patanjali, in his Yoga Aphorisms, one of the most extraordinary documents of ancient science known to the world. Here must have been the home of that learning which made the golden age of the Guptas possible, between 300 and 500 A.D. We must think too of the international relations of these ancient monastic colleges. Fa Hian (400 A.D.) and Hiuen Tsang (650 A.D.) were not the only eastern students who came in the ages that followed the Christian era to drink of tbe springs of Indian learning. They were a couple whose books of travels happen to have become famous. But they were two out of a great procession of pilgrim-scholars. And it was to the abbeys that such came. It was from these abbeys, again, that the missions proceeded to foreign countries. No nation was ever evangelised by a single teacher. The word Patrick in Irish, it is said, means praying-man, and the vaunted saint is thus, beyond a doubt, either a member or a personification of a whole race of Christian preachers who carried Baptism and the Cross to early Ireland. Similarly Mahinda, Nagarjuna, and Bodhidharma in the twelfth century, were not the isolated figures painted by history as we know it. They were merely conspicuous elements in a whole stream of missionary effort, that radiated from the quiet abbeys and monasteries of India in its great ages towards the worlds of east and west. Christianity itself, has been often suggested, may have been one of the later fruits of such a mission, as preached in Persia and Syria.

Here, in these lovely retreats—for they are all placed in the midst of natural beauty-was elaborated the thought and learning, the power of quiet contemplation, and the marvellous energy of art and literary tradition, that have made India as we know her today. Here were dreamed those dreams which, reflected in society, became the social ideals of the ages in which we live. And here was demonstrated the great law that will be expressed again and again in history, whenever the glory of India rises to one of its supreme moments, the law of the antithesis between city and university, between Samaj and religious orders, between the life of affairs and the life of thought. Antithetic as they are, however, these are nevertheless complementary. Spirituality brings glory in its train. The monastic life reacts to make civic strength.

●●●

12

RAJGIR: AN ANCIENT BABYLON

Up, up, up. The long array of steps seems endless, as we climb the steep hillside to reach the dwelling that has been lent us for a few weeks' habitation; and, after all, when we come upon it, it is nothing but a nest of robber-barons, this old manor-house of the Rajas of Annwa. A nest of robber-barons, truly, perched half-way up the mountain and concealed from sight, and yet with a wide stretch of country well in its own purview. Curiously small and unfortified to Western thinking, it consists of two parts a court on the inside guarded against intrusion and crowned with wide terrace-roofs; and without, a few rooms ranged about two sides of an open square. Its feudal and mediaeval character lends the building interest which its undeniable beauty well sustains. But far beyond either of these considerations is the exciting fact that we are to keep house for twenty-one days in a spot where for a period of from twenty-five to thirty centuries there has been continuously a human habitation. For the great staircase by which we have climbed the rugged hillside is undoubtedly constructed over the foundations of the ancient walls of Rajgir, and the earliest predecessor of the Barons of Annwa must have chosen for his family stronghold to develop one of the buttresses of the guardroom of the selfsame walls, occurring on a small plateau. Below us lies the floor of the winding pass with the stream that forms a moat at the foot of our mountain-stairway. In front a great curving staircase, constituting what our modern railway companies would call a loop of the fort, protects those temples and hot springs of Rajgir which still form the objective of a yearly Hindu pilgrimage. And out in the open, a stone's throwaway as it seems in this clear plain atmosphere, but really perhaps a mile by the road, is the modern village of Rajgir, ancient Raja-griha, the city or dwelling-place of kings.

Already the villagers are showing us friendly attentions. The servant who has come with us was born a few miles away, and his womenfolk are arriving with our first meal in hospitable readiness. The peasant-guards have established themselves in the outer rooms for our protection, and a small boy of the neighbourhood is clamouring to be taken on as an attendant. It is as if we were guests of Semiramis in Nineveh of old It is like pitching our tent on the ruins of Babylon and entering into friendly relations wth lineal descendants of the ancient inhabitants.

How beautiful is the country that lies stretched before us! Outward from the mouth of our twisting pass, at Christmas time or thereabouts, it will be covered in the green of rice and other crops, with every here and there a field of white opium poppies in full bloom. But now, at the change of the season in October, we see here fields as patches of many-coloured earth—purple and brown and red—and we remember the words of Buddha, half laughing doubtless yet full of affectionate memory and tenderness, of one who said to a disciple in a much-patched garment that he reminded him of the ricefields about Rajgir.

A quarter of a mile behind us the hills open out into a circle, and here lie the ruins of the ancient city of kings—wondedully clear and distinct in every part of them. We almost might trace out the very lines of the bazaars. With regard to streets and roads, it sounds dangerously near truism to say that they retain their positions with little change from age to age; yet I do not know that the fact has been much noted. Here in Rajgir at any rate, where hundreds of cows and buffaloes, sheep and goats, are driven daily by the herds to and from the ancient ruins, many of the main roadways remain much as they must have been in the dim past. Here, for instance, is the thoroughfare that ran through the city, with traces at a certain point near the cenre of the palace walls, bastions, and gateways; and here beyond the palace are the outlines of the royal pleasure-grounds, with their wonderfully engineered ornamental waters intact to this day.

All through this little mountain arena and the pass that leads to it, indeed, there has been an extraordinary amount of hydraulic engineering. It would seem as if the fame of the hot springs must have been the original cause of the royal settlement in this natural fortress, and the artificial development of its streams the main occupation of the kingly line thereafter. Even now below our own walled and moated manor lies an empty tank that two thousand years ago most likely held lotuses in a park. Even now the river that runs through the valley, though naturally one, is divided in parts into two and even three streams, forming a network that is enough to show us the attention that must have been paid in ancient India to the problems of irrigation, in order to give birth to so marvellous a degree of hydraulic science. Far away in Central India is a monumental building, of an age some two hundred years later than that of old Rajgir, which shows by its ornamental cascades the same engineering genius and the same royal idea of beauty and magnificence as we find here. Well may the Indian people glory in the ancestry which already lived in this splendour, while that of Northern and Western Europe went dad in painted wood.

There can be a few places in the world so old as Rajgir, about which so much is definitely known and so much safely to be inferred. It was in all probability about the year 590 B.C.—in a world in which Babylon and Phoenicia and Egypt and Sheba were of all facts most living and important—it was about the yeal 590 B.C. that there came along the road leading into the valley yonder, one whose very form was radiant with feeling and thought, that lifted him above the common world into that consciousness that makes history.

It may have been early morning when He came. For the books say that the great company of goats was being led up at that moment for the royal sacrifice; fixed, it may have been, for about the hour of noon. Or it may have been about the time of cowdust, on the eve of the festival, and the herdsmen may have intended to stable their goats for that night outside the palace. In any case He came, some say carrying on his shoulder a lame kid, followed by the patter of thousands of little hoofs. He came, moreover, in a passion of pity. A veritable storm of compassion had broken loose within him on behalf of these, the helpless "little brothers" of humanity, who were caught like man himself in the net of pain and pleasure, of life and death; bewildered like man by love and sorrow, but who unlike man for want of speech could neither express their perplexity nor form a conception of release. Surely they crowded round Him, and rubbed themselves against Him again and again, the gentle, wondering, four-footed things!

For the animals are strangely susceptible to the influence of a silent love that has no designs on their life or freedom. All the legends of the world tell us that they catch the hush of Christmas Eve, respond to the eager questioning of the child Dhruva, and understand that unmeasured yearning to protect them which may be read in the eyes of the Lord Buddha on the road that goes up to the palace of Rajgir.

We had been some time in the place before we noticed that it was on one particular islet in the river below us that the village deathfires might so often be seen at evening. It was a very ancient custom in India to burn the dead by the stream side just outside the town. But this sandbank was far away from the village. Hardly could they have chosen a point less easily accessible. Ah, yes! certainly there was the explanation; the burning ghat of these peasants in the twentieth century must be still where their ancestors had chosen it, in the fifth, in the first—aye, even for centuries before that—may be immediately without the city of old Rajgir. It takes a peculiar angle of vision, and perhaps a peculiar mood of passivity, to see the trees turn into a forest when the existence of such was previously unsuspected. So I shall not attempt to guess how many more evenings elapsed before, as we went along the roadway on the far side of the burning ghat, one of us noted the broken steps and the entwined tamarind and Bo-trees that marked the old-time ghat of Rajgir. Nor do I know how many more days went by before there came to some one of us the flash of insight that led us finally to discover that the mass of fallen masonry close by was that very ancient gateway of the city through which Buddha himself with the goats must have passed, and brought to our notice the dome-like head of an old Stupa lying in the dust a few feet away.

Passing through the gate and standing at the opening of the theatre-like valley, we find that the river which flows out of the city as one, is made up of two streams which between them encircle the royal city as a moat, even within its girdle of mountains and its enclosing walls. They join at this point. Leaving unexplored that which flows towards us from the left part of the garden of Ambapali, the Indian Mary Magdalene, and past the abodes of many of the characters who figure in the narrative of Buddha's life, we may turn to that branch which comes to us from the right.

A world of discoveries awaits us here! The path leads us across to the water, but this is easily forded by stepping-stones which may still be detected as fragments of an ancient bathing ghat. Evidently bathing and the bathing-ghat were as prominent in the Indian civilisation twenty-five centuries ago as they are today. Then the road follows the streamside at a distance of some fifty yards more or less from the line of mountains on the right. About midway through the city the face of this mountain is pierced by a great cave, known today to the peasants of the countryside as the Sone Bhandar or Golden Treasury. The interior of this cave is polished, not carved. There stands in it, as if some party of robbers had been interrupted in an attempt to carry it away, the earliest Stupa I have ever seen. The outside is half concealed by shrubs and creepers. But even now the mortice-holes remain that show where the carved wooden ornaments were once attached. And even now, as we stand at the entrance, we see in the distance, in the middle of the city, the tower that Fa Hian noted as still intact and visible in the year A.D. 404, crowning a small Stupa or well to the east of the palace.

This cave then was the cathedral of old Rajgir. Here Buddha must have rested or meditated or taught: and there must, suggested some member of our party, have been a roadway connecting it directly with the palace. Acting on this clue, we proceeded to brush aside the wild growths and explore the line between the two. Outside the cave we found a level floor of ancient asphalt, a sort of Venetian Plaza de San Marco as it were. This was evidently the town square. We read a reference in one of the old Chinese Suttas of a certain place in Rajgir—as "the place where the peacocks were fed" ; how our minds had lingered over the words when we first read them! And now here we stand. For undoubtedly just as the pigeons are fed outside St. Paul's so on this asphalt plaza, before the cathedral entrance in Eastern city, it fitted the royal dignity and bounty that peacocks should be daily given grain.

The asphalt runs down to the river and across it. For the water still flows under the ancient bridge, and we can walk on it though its level is somewhat sunken. Easily, then, we make our way to the royal mansion, clearly marked as this is at its four corners by the foundations of four bastion towers. But turning again to the bridge, we find an unbroken line of this same asphalt running along the bank by the way we have come, though sooth to say we might never have noticed it if we had not been tracing it out from the conspicuous mass.

Was this, the river-front opposite to the palace, protected by the steep hills behind, and running, from the town plaza to the bathing-ghat beyond, and across this to the city gates—was this the High Street of the ancient town? Every now and again, as day after day we pace brooding up and down the distance, every now and again we come upon some hitherto unnoticed mass of masonry or mason's tool-marks. Here are a couple of blocks lying on their sides, as if to form a seat in a river-wall. Here again traces of steps or fallen ornaments. At one place on the opposite bank, deeply sunk between masses of earth and vegetation, there runs down to the riverside a small ravine that would now pass as a gully if the pavement or ancient asphalt did not prove it—in days before Pompeii and Herculaneum were born—to have been a street.

What were the houses like that looked down upon these footways? What was the life that was lived in them? How long had the place been a city? How long did it continue to be one? What were the surroundings in the height of its glory of this abode of kings, now an austere and desolate ruin? These and a thousand other questions crowd upon us, and it is strange to how many of them we can give an answer. The rushing rains of Indian summers have long washed away most of the soil from the hanging gardens that once clothed the hillsides, and made the prospect from the palace to the gates and beyond them through the pass leading out into the plains a veritable vision of delight.

But still the artificial terraces of red trap-rock are smooth and level amidst the out-cropping masses of natural crags, and still the wanderer may take his stand on some spot whence Bimbisara, the king, was wont to look upon the glories of his inheritance, or, with difficulty at one or two points, may trace the way through the old pleasance by which doubtless royal hunting-parties may have started for the forest-glades. Today, it is true, there are no rich woodlands covering slopes and mountain-tops, as in the royal ages. Wild undergrowth, dense shrubs, and here and there a twisted palm growing in a cranny are all that can stand for the lofty timbers, dense aisles of the days when the place was a paradise, a king's garden surrounding a king's palace. And still at the back of the ruined city, guarding it from the passes on the south and east, we find the double walls of enormous thickness.

The square mortice-holes in the face of the rock out of which the great Sone Bhandar is hollowed, give us a clue that enables us to rebuild, mentally, the ancient city. For these mortice-holes held the attachments of the wooden ornaments that formed the front of the cave. Now, between Bombay and Poona, on the west of India, is another cave, that of Karle, which though of a much later date, must be of the same style and period as this, and there the wooden front is still intact. Moreover, the carvings form a picture, as Fergusson has pointed out, of an ancient street, from which we gather that the second storeys of houses standing in rows were decorated in front with crowded wooden verandahs, porches, niches, and all sorts of beautiful and irregular curved corners. That these, further, were not mere devices of beauty in the case of the houses, as they were in those of the caves, we see in the pictures which were carved, probably in the first or second century A.D., on the gateways of Sanchi. From these we can gather an idea of what the palace of Bimbisara and the homes of his subjects must have been like.

The first storey, then, was massive, sloping inwards and upwards, loopholed and buttressed at its four corners by four circular towers. The first storey only was built of stone, and its parapet was battlemented. On the strong terrace provided by the roof of this fortification were constructed the family living rooms, which were of wood and much carved. That it would have been possible, however, to withdraw the women into the lower storey in time of war may be seen from buried ruins at Ujjain, which are shown by the Pandas as part of Vikramaditya's palace, and appear to have belonged to a fortress of Asoka's time. Here, built of hard grey stone, now black with age, we have what seems to be the inside corner, and part of the courtyard, of just such a building as the Sanchi sculptures would lead us to expect as the dwelling of a king or noble.

Outside, the walls would be almost blind; inside, they are honeycombed with many-pillared halls and verandahs, and one room with raised floor that represents an old Indian form of bedchamber and bed in one. In times of peace these were, we may suppose, the quarters assigned to men-at-arms. The building is of a massiveness that rivals nature, and there are a few pillars still left–amongst the many that the succeeding sovereigns decorated in different degrees and different styles—whose simplicity of form enables any observer that knows Sanchi to feel fairly confident in assigning the building as a whole to the reign of Asoka, or earlier.

Of such a form, then, though perhaps smaller and less elaborate, may we suppose the palace of Rajgir to have been, and in the streets about it the more plebeian dwellings of the townsfolk must, though small and comparatively huddled, have been like unto it. True, their lower storeys would be built, in all probability, even as the huts of the Rajgir pilgrims are to this day, of mud and pebbles, instead of lordly stone. From hillocks formed of such deposits, anyone may pick out by the streamside, at various different levels, bits of old household pottery. But the facings and tops of the shops and houses were doubtless of carved wood, and the front of the cathedral was a faithful enough reflex of the life of the town. Through such streets, while the king stood watching him from the roof of the palace, paced the Sakya Prince, "a lad in his first youth," ere yet he was Buddha, and no honour that Bimbisara could offer would tempt him from that bridal of Poverty in which alone his mind delighted. "This life of the household is pain, free only is he who lives in the open air"; thinking thus he embraced the life of the wandering monk.

Far away from Rajgir, in the north of Rajputana we have Amber and Jaipur, a couple of cities which every visitor to India tries to see. Of these, Amber is situated in the highlands, and Jaipur out in the plain, Amber being, of course, very much the older of the two. It is in fact an old Indian doctrine that no city should occupy the same ground for more than a thousand years. It is supposed that a potent means of avoiding pestilence and other ills is to move out and occupy a new space. In accordance with this canon the new city of Jaipur was laid out. And when all was finished, the Maharaja moved into the new town with all his people.

Now this history of Amber and Jaipur, enacted in modern India and still fresh in the memory of the Rajput people, is our guide to much in the history of old Rajgir. For in the lifetime of Buddha, the son of Bimbisara—that tragic king, Ajatasatru, across whose path falls the red shadow of a father's murder!—found that the time had come to move the city of kings, and he accordingly built a new city with walls and gates like the last but out in the open plain. And there the grass-covered ruin lies to this day, to the west of the present village, the grave of a city, the memorial of new Rajgir.

Bimbisara was the king of Magadha in the days of the Great Renunciation. Ajatasatru was king at the death of Buddha. But we know, from the fact of the desertion of their highland stronghold and its rebuilding outside, that for five hundred years at least before their time there had been a city on the site of old Rajgir.

Nor need we think that the city thus built was only a palace and its appurtenances. The fact that it actually became the new centre of population, forming the direct ancestor of the present village, shows itself two hundred years later, when the great Asoka, desiring to build fitting memorials to Him whom the emperor delighted to honour, chose its north-western corner, on the left hnd of the main gateway, whereat to place a Stupa and Asokan pillar with an inscription. As the edicts carved by Asoka on rocks and pillars have the character of proclamations, it follows that the rocks and pillars themselves partake somewhat of the nature of the modern journal, inasmuch as they were the means adopted to publish the royal will, and hence a position could never be selected for them at a distance from inhabited cities. The inscribed pillar at Sarnath was placed at the door or in the courtyard of a monastery. And similarly the inscribed pillars, whose fragments have been found at Pataliputra, were erected in the interior or on the site of the old jail as an act of imperial penance.

We may take it, then, that old Rajgir was really deserted at about the time of Bimbisara's successor, and, if it was afterwards used as a royal residence, was so used at intervals, as Amber is now. Such then was the city, already ancient, through which Buddha himself had passed time and again and where He was held by all as an honourable guest. Across these fields and up and down these streets, now ruined, or within the massive cathedral-cave of Sone Bhandar, there echo to this hour the immortal reverberations of Buddha's voice.

Why did He come this way at all? Was it for the sake of the learned men who forgather in the neighbourhood of capitals? Was the famous university of Nalanda of after-ages already perhaps. a university, where one might come in the sure hope of finding all the wisdom of the age? It would seem as if, any way, He passed this spot with treasure already in the heart, needing only long years of brooding thought to fuse his whole

Self in its realisation. Unless He was sure of the truth before He reached here, He could not have gone, sure and straight as an arrow from the bow, to the unfrequented forest of bael-trees, with its cave overhanging the river, and its great tree between the farms and ponds, where now the humble village of Bodh-Gaya stands.

•••

13

CHINA CAME TO LEARN

Amongst Indian historical documents there is none more fascinating than the books of their travels written by the early Chinese pilgrims. Of these the two now best known to us are those of Faltian, who came to India about A.D. 400, and Hiuen Tsang, about A.D 640. Hiuen Tsang, owing partly to the accident that his life was afterwards written by his disciples, appears to us as a personality, as the head and master of a large religious following, as a saint as well as a scholar, a monk as well as a traveller. But Fa-Hian is a lonelier, more impersonal figure. Monk and pilgrim as he was, it is rather the geographer that impresses us in him. Grave and sparing of words, he tells us little or nothing of himself. For all we know, he may have been the very first of the travellers who came to India on the task of Buddhistic research. From the surprise with which he is everywhere received and the complimentary exclamations that he records, it would appear indeed as if this had been so.

On the other hand, from the quietness with which he comes and goes, from his silence about royal favours, and his own freedom from self-consciousness, **it would seem as if the sight of Chinese visitors had not been rare in the India of that period**, though the errand on which he and his party had come might single them out for some special degree of reverence and interrogation. "How great must be the devotion of these priests," said the people in the Punjab, "that they should have come thus to learn the law from the very extremity of the earth!" And yet frequent references to "the Clergy of Reason" in Kosala and in the south, these Clergy of Reason having apparently been Taoist monks on pilgrimage, involve a curious contradiction in this matter. Hiuen Tsang's is really a work of autobiography, but Fa-Hian's is rather the abstract of a statement made before some learned society, perhaps a university in the south of China, and countersigned by them.

In a certain year, with certain companions, Fa-Hian set out to make search in India for the Laws and Precepts of Religion, "because he had been distressed in Chhang'an (Sian in Shen-si, evidently his native province) to observe the Precepts and the theological works on the point of being lost, and already disfigured by lacunae." Such are the quiet words with which the narrative begins. So colourless can be the phrases in which the passion of a life is stated. From that moment when Fa-Hian set out, to that other day when "at the end of the summer rest, they went out to meet Fa-Hian the traveller", who had surmounted obstacles incredible, and borne difficulties innumerable, was to be fifteen long years!

His book consists of some forty short chapters or paragraphs, each one dealing as a rule with a separate province or country. Of it he himself says:

"The present is a mere summary. Not having been heard by the Masters hitherto, he (Fa-Hian) casts not his eyes retrospectively on details. He crossed the sea and hath returned, after having overcome every manner of fatigue, and has enjoyed the happiness of receiving many high and noble favours. He has been in dangers, and has escaped them. And now therefore he puts upon the bamboo what has happened to him, anxious to communicate to the wise what he hath seen and heard."•

We can hardly doubt that this is a form of superscription, offering his paper on his travels to the consideration of some organised body of scholars.

Those travels themselves had occupied fifteen years. From the leaving of his native province of Chhang'an till his crossing of the Indus, "the river in the west", was a six years' journey. He spent six years in India itself, including two in Orissa. And finally, reckoning apparently two years spent in Ceylon, he was three years on the voyage home. Each stage of the journey is described, from the time of leaving Chhang'an. The kingdoms which he has traversed, he says in closing, number at least thirty. But, though the provinces south and west of Khotan are called "India of the North", he scarcely seems to think that he has reached India proper till he comes to Mathura. This he treats almost as if it were a capital. He seizes the moment of his arrival there to give one of his gem-like pictures of the whole country and its civilisation. He describes the Government, the freedom with which men come and go, untroubled by passport regulations, and the self-restraint with which justice is administered and the criminal punished. We must remember that these were the times of Vikramaditya, said to have been "of Ujjain".

Was Ujjain, perhaps, the name of all Western India, and Mathura its metropolis? Compared with Mathura, Pataliputra appears relatively unimportant. It was older, grayer perhaps, and more imposing. It had been "the capital of Asoka". Its palaces were still marvellous. Ecclesiastically, too, it was strong as well as noted. Royal delegates were posted there from each of the provinces. But commercially, and perhaps even politically also, we feel that the centre of power in India was at the time of Fa-Hian's visit at Mathura. From this he makes his way, by Samkassa and Kanauj, into the heart of Buddha's own country -Sravasti, Kapilavastu, Kushinagara, and so on, down to Ganga, a chain of sites that by the painstaking labours of so many archaeologists have now been in great measure recovered. From Ganga he returns to Pataliputra, and thence makes his way to Banaras and Kausambi. Again making Pataliputra his headquarters, he seems to have spent three years in the Buddha country learning Sanskrit and copying manuscripts. And finally he sailed down the Ganga, through the kingdom of Champa, and came to Tamluk, or Tamralipti, where he stayed two years. When he left Tamralipti in a large ship for the south-west, he appears to have reckoned himself, though he was yet to spend two years in Ceylon, as already on the return journey.

The journey, as he describes it, constitutes an abstract of all that concerns Buddhism, and quietly ignores everything else in the country. "Brahmanas and heretics" is Fa-Hian's comprehensive term for Hinduism in all its non-Buddhistic phases. We are able to gather a great deal nevertheless about the state of the country from his pages. In the first place we learn—as we do with still greater emphasis later from Hiuen Tsang—that to a learned Chinese, who had made an exhaustive study of Buddhism in Gandhara, and the kingdoms of the north-west frontier, India proper, or "India of the Middle", as he calls it, was still the country in which to seek for original and authentic images. Traversing Gandhara, Swat, Darada, Udyana, Takshashila, Purushapura, and Nagara (probably Kabul), it was not in any of these, but in Tamralipti that our traveller spent two years copying books and painting images.

Again, already, at the time of Fa-Hian's visit, the old city of Rajgir, he tells us, is "entirely desert and uninhabited." It follows that the carvings and statuary in which to this day that site is rich are to a great extent of a school of sculpture which had grown, flourished, and decayed prior to A.D. 400. This in itself is a fact of immense importance. We constantly find in the travels that sacred places are marked by "chapels, monasteries, and Stupas". Now a chapel of Buddha is undoubtedly an image-house. Nor is Fa-Hian himself entirely without feeling for the historical aspect of that Buddhistic sculpture which is one of the chosen objects of his study. He speaks always as if images were common enough in Buddhism, but he tells us that "the first of all images of Buddha, and that which men in aftertimes have copied," was a certain bull's head carved in sandal-wood, which was made by Prasenajit, king of Kosala, at the time when Buddha was in the Tusita heaven preaching to his mother.

The difference between an image and an emblem does not seem here to be very clearly apprehended, but the statement shows once for all that men in the fourth and fifth centuries looked to the eastern provinces, and to the country of Buddha's own activity, as the historic source of Buddhistic statuary. Again, when travelling in the kingdom of Tho-Iy—north-east of the Indus, east of Afghanistan, and south of the Hindu Kush; or, as has been suggested, Darada of the Dards—he tells us that there was once an Arhat in this kingdom who sent a certain sculptor to the Tusita heaven to study the stature and features of Maitreya Bodhisattva. Three times the man went, and when he came down he made an image of heroic size, about eight English feet in height, which on festival days was wont to become luminous, and to which neighbouring kings rendered periodic worship.

"This image," adds the pilgrim, in the far-away tone of one who speaks on hearsay, "still exists in the same locality." It was after the making of this statue, he further tells us, that the Buddhist missionaries began to come from the far side of the Indus, with their collections of the books and of the Sacred Precepts; and the image was erected. three hundred years after the

Mahanirvana. Here we learn a great deal. In the first place, when Buddhism crossed the Indus, three hundred years after the death of Buddha, it was already the religion of the Bodhisattvas. Obviously there had been solitary saints, and perhaps even communities of monastics, without the books before—or how should there have been an Arhat to transport a sculptor three times to the Tusita heaven?—but there was a sudden accession of Buddhistic culture at a date three hundred years after the death of the Master, and this culture was Mahayanist in character. Thus the Mahayana doctrine with its fully-equipped pantheon, its images, and its collections of books, to be declared canonical under Kanishka purported to come, like the Hinayana, from India proper, or, as Fa-Hian calls it, Madhyadesha. Magadha, Kosala, and Vaishali, then, may claim the honour of having initiated Buddhistic art as fully and truly as Buddhistic thought.

Further, it is clear that in Magadha itself the great ages of sculpture were felt to be already past. Talking of Pataliputra, which had been the capital of Asoka, "the palaces in the town have walls," says our traveller, "of which the stones were put together by genii. The sculptures and the carved work which adorn the windows are such as cannot be equalled in the present age. They still exist." We who have seen the work done under Mogul emperors in marble, and the pierced sandstones of modern Banaras, might not, had we seen them also, have been so ready as Fa-Hian to attribute a supernatural origin to the window of the Asokan palaces. But the fact remains that an unimpeachable witness has assured us of the greatness and beauty of such work in Magadha, with the reputation of being ancient at the beginning of the fifth century A.D.

The great difficulty in the path of Fa-Hian was the scarcity of written documents. Everywhere he inquired for books, he tells us, but everywhere he found that the precepts were handed down by memory from master to disciple, each book having its given professor. At last, in the great temple of Victory in the Buddha country he found what he wanted, and there he stayed three years to copy. This is a most important light on many questions besides that with which it deals. **It accounts, as nothing else could have done, for the tenacity with which the pure doctrine of Buddhism seems to have been held for so many centuries. The concentration of energy necessary for the carrying out of such a task as the memorising of a vast literature explains the gravity and decorum of the Orders so long maintained.** "The decency, the gravity, the piety of the clergy," meaning the Buddhist monks, Fa-Hian takes several occasions to say, "are admirable. They cannot be described."

It explains the tendency of Buddhistic monasteries to become universities. It explains the synthetic tendencies of the faith, which in the time of Kanishka could already include eighteen schools of doctrine declared to be mutually compatible, and not defiant. It also explains, turning to another subject altogether, why the first written version of the old Puranas should always so evidently be an edited version of an ancient original. It visualises for us the change from Pali to Sanskrit, and it justifies the sparseness of written archives in matters of Indian history. These were evidently memorised. On this point indeed Fa-Hian constantly tells us that kings. granting lands to the Buddhistic orders engrave their deeds on iron, and we can only feel that as. long as this was so, their non-survival is not to be wondered at. It must have been at a comparatively later period that brass and copper came to be used for a similar purpose, with the desired effect of permanence. Curiously enough, in Tamralipti there is no mention of difficulty regarding manuscripts. Nor again in Ceylon. In the last-named kingdom we know that the writing down had begun at least two or three centuries before the visit of Fa-Hian, and he would seem to have benefited by this fact. We gather then that as Magadha and Kosala were the source of Buddhistic doctrine in its different phases, and the source of successive waves of Buddhistic symbolism. so also they were the first religion to feel the impulse of a literary instead of a verbal transmission of the canonical scriptures.

The difference between "India of the North"—or the Gandharan provinces beyond the Indus—and India proper in all matters of learning and the faith comes out very prominently in the pages of Fa-Hian, and ought to refute sufficiently all who imagine Gandhara as possessed of a culture in any way primary and impulsive, instead of entirely derivative and passive.

As if forecasting our need on this very point, the pilgrim particularly notes that on reaching India proper (and apparently in the great temple of Chhi'honan or Victory in Kosala) his last remaining companion, Tao-chhing, when he "beheld the law of the Shaneen, and all the clergy grave, decorous, and conducting themselves in a manner greatly to be admired, reflected, with a sigh, that the inhabitants of the frontiers of the kingdom of Thsin (China) were deficient in Precepts and transgressed their duties; and said that if hereafter he could become Buddha, he wished that he might not be reborn in the country of the frontiers; on this account he remained, and returned not. Fa-Hian, whose first desire was that the Precepts should be diffused and should penetrate into the land of Han, returned therefore alone."

About this same "India of the North" we have still more detail. The pre-Buddhistic Buddhism, which undoubtedly existed and was represented in Buddha's own day by his cousin Devadatta, was much more living in the Gandharan provinces at the time of Fa-Hian's journey than in India proper. Also the Birth Stories had become the romance of these provinces, and there were Stupas there to the almsgiving of the eyes and of the head, to the giving of his own flesh by the Bodhisattva to redeem a dove, and to the making himself a meal for the starving tigress.

We cannot help distinguishing between those countries whose Buddhism was Hinayana and those in which it was Mahayana, as more or less anciently the goal of Buddhist missions. And we note that Udyana, whose name seems to indicate that it had been a royal residence, perhaps the home country, as it were, of the Kushan dynasty, was entirely Mahayana, and is mentioned under the name of Ujjana, as one of the northern Tirthas[1] in the Mahabharata. It would appear, indeed, that when the Himavant began to be parcelled out into a series of Mahabharata stations some time under the later Guptas, the undertaking was in direct and conscious succession to an earlier appropriation of the regions further west, as stations of the Jatakas, or Birth Stories of Buddha. We ought not, in the attempt to follow up some of the thousand and one threads of interest that our traveller leaves for us, to forget the one or two glimpses of himself that he vouchsafes us. Never can one who has read it forget the story of his visit to the cave that he knew on the hill of Gridhrakuta, where Buddha used to meditate, in old Rajgir:

"Fa-Hian, having purchased in the new town perfumes, flowers, and oil lamps, hired two aged Bhikshus to conduct him to the grots and to the hill Khi-che. Having made an oblation of the perfumes and the flowers, the lamps increased the brilliance. Grief and emotion affected him even to tears. He said, 'Formerly in this very place was Buddha. Here he taught the Sheou-leng-yan.[1] Fa-Hian, unable to behold Buddha in life, has but witnessed the traces of his sojourn. Still, it is something to have recited the Sheou-leng-yan before the cave, and to have dwelt there one night."

But Fa-Hian, enthusiast as he was, and capable of extreme exertions in the cause 'of the Faith and China,

1. The things which are difficult to discriminate from one another.

was not this alone. There was also in that grave and modest nature a chord that vibrated to the thought of home. "He longed ardently," he says, when he had already reached the South of China, "to see Chhang'an again, but, that which he had at heart being a weighty matter, he halted in the South where the masters published the Sacred Books and the Precepts." Thus he excuses himself for a brief delay on the way back to his native province. But if he feels thus when he has already landed on Chinese shores, what must have been his longing while still in foreign lands? In Ceylon, seated before the blue jasper image of Buddha, perhaps at Anuradhapuram, he pauses to tell us:

"Many years had now elapsed since Fa-Hian left the land of Han. The people with whom he mingled were men of foreign lands. The hills, the rivers, the plants, the trees, everything that had met his eyes was strange to him. And what was more, those who had begun the journey with him were now separated from him. Some had remained behind, and some had died. Ever reflecting on the past, his heart was thoughtful and dejected. Suddenly. while at the side of this jasper figure, he beheld a merchant presenting in homage to it a fan of white lute-string of the country of Tsin. Without anyone's perceiving it, this excited so great an emotion that the tears flowed and filled his eyes. "

Nor can we forget the simple and beautiful countersignature which seems to have been affixed by the learned body to whom he presented it, to Fa-Hian's written summary of his travels. After telling how they met Fa-Hian and discoursed with him, interrogating him, and after telling how his words inspired trust, his good faith lent confidence to his recital, the scribe of the Chinese University, or Secretary to the Imperial Geographical Society, as it may have been ("the masters" in any case he calls them), ends thus:

"They were touched with these words. They were touched to behold such a man: they observed amongst themselves that a very few had indeed expatriated themselves for the sake of the Doctrine, but no one had ever forgotten self in quest of the law, as Fa-Hian had done. One must know the conviction which truth produces, otherwise one cannot partake of the zeal which produces earnestness. Without merit and without activity, nothing is achieved. On accomplishing aught, with merit and with activity, how shall one be abandoned to oblivion? To lose what is esteemed—to esteem what mankind forgot—Oh!'

●●●

14

LAND OF JOYFUL SAGAS

Unseen, but all-pervasive, in the life of every community, is the great company of the ideals. No decalogue has half the influence over human conduct that is exercised by a single drama or a page of narrative. The theory of chivalry interests us, but the Idylls of the King help to mould our character.

The whole of history, in so far as it may be known, is the common possession of the race; but, in addition to this, every language makes its own contribution of literary creations, and national custom determines the degree in which these shall become available to all classes of the community, thereby reacting upon the national type. Few have considered how much might be done to ennoble and dignify common life in England by a wider dispersion of the love for Shakespeare. As it is, the Bible being the only book that is used in this sense, the careers and opinions of a few Syrian shepherds are apt to be more potent among us than that of great Brutus, Desdemona, Horatio, and their kindred, who are offspring of the genius of our countryman; and in some sense, therefore, the fruit of English civic life itself.

It is said that in Greece the poetry of Homer and Euripides is known amongst the poorer classes to this day; and certain it is that the Catholic Church has done a great and little-understood service in bringing the lives of the saints of all countries to bear upon the development of each. Every man habitually measures himself against some model; therefore every addition to the range of available types is to be welcomed. A king feels himself to be one of a class of royal persons who must be not only authoritative but also picturesque in their behaviour.- And, whether he likes it or not, by this standard he knows himself to stand or fall. His very rank forces his pattern upon him. Amongst those of smaller place and greater personal freedom, capacity more readily shows its own complexion. Some of us—were our common place faculties touched with divine fire—would find our destiny in the qualities of the ideal merchant and administrator.

That peculiar form of integrity, dignity, and wisdom that belongs to such a function would prove to be ours, or attainable by us. But although this is probably the commonest logical issue in English national life at present, it does not follow that every Englishman is fitted to achieve it. Here and there, especially perhaps among the Celtic contingent, we find one born for the quite different goal of perfect knighthood. Loyalty to leader and comrade, sympathy for the oppressed, far-shining fearlessness and love of freedom, are traits characteristic of an age of chivalry; and persons who embody them represent such a period, it being neither more nor less admirable than that of merchant-prince and caravan-chief.

The potentialities of one man lead towards sainthood, of another to poetry, of a third to science or mechanics. One gravitates into leadership, another as naturally becomes disciple. One enjoys knowledge, another ignorance.

Were all of us developed to our own utmost, we may take it that every place in life would be filled, every part in the world-drama played, but by men and women of such ripe and determined personality that we could no more confuse one with the other than we could mistake the conduct of Helen of Troy for that of Elisabeth of Hungary, or hers for that of Faust's Gretchen.

We have to notice, moreover, that in European life only the born idealist is deeply influenced by any of the miscellaneous characters of history and literature. Religion alone amongst us can exercise this compelling power on a large scale. And this is related to the fact that only religion gives ideals themselves as motives. Circumstances have in many cases offered such a setting that a life has been forced into brilliance and distinction, but the self-born intention of the saints could never be wholly fulfilled. Iphigenia could hardly have refused her sacrifice. Joan of Arc, on the contrary, must always have felt that the sword of Michael might have been held still more stainless and with a greater courage. It is this fact that gives to the ideals of religion their supreme power of individuation. We must remember also that they differ from others in making a universal appeal. The girl who aimed at becoming Portia would be guilty of vanity: she whose model is the Blessed Virgin receives the respect of all. To imitate Socrates would be a miserable. affectation; to imitate the religious hero is regarded as a common duty.

It may seem impossible to dower the heroes and heroines of literature with this projective energy of the lives of saints; but in India, as to some extent in Iceland, the feat has been accomplished. For, India is also one of the saga-lands. **At every lull in her history we may hear the chanting of her bards, the joy of her people in the story of their past.** The long twllight of the North is no better adapted to the growth of such a literature than the deep and early night of the South. In verandahs and courtyards, with the women concealed behind screens at the back, it has been the Indian fashion for hundreds of years through the winter months to gather at dusk round the seat of the Wandering Teller, and listen hour after hour to his stirring theme. Surrounded by lights and flowers, gay carpets and burning incense, there is in his performance a mixture of reading, song, and story. It is something of opera, sermon, and literature all in one.

Ever since the commencement of our era the Hindu people have possessed in their present forms two great poems, the Mahabharata and the Ramayana. The first of these is their Wars of Troy, their Heimskringla, their Marte d'Arthur. That is to say, it is the book of the Deeds and the Wars of the Heroes. Thanks to the long-established culture of the race, and the prestige which all literature enjoys as "sacred", the Mahabharata is to this day the strongest influence in the shaping of the lives and ambitions of Hindu boys.

The battle which it describes took place, if at all, very nearly fifteen hundred years before the birth of Christ. It lasted many days, and the field of combat was called Kurukshetra, being situated on that great plain near Delhi where critical moments in the history of India have been so often decided. For many a century after Kurukshetra the wandering bards all over India sang of the great battle; and when any new theme claimed their creative powers, it had to be recounted as if originally told by one of the heroes to another at some particular moment in the course of the main narrative. In this way the heart's heart of the whole poem, the Bhagavad-Gita brings an interesting instance of double drama with it. The Gita consists in itself of a dialogue between a young Chieftain and Krishna, the Divine Personage who is acting as his charioteer, at the moment of the opening of the eighteen days' combat. But the device which enables the conversation to be given in detail is the picture of an old blind king, head of one of the rival houses, seated some miles away, and attended in his anxiety by a man of what is called Yogic, or hyper aesthetic, that is, psychic sense, who utters to him every word as it is spoken.

The exquisite story of Savitri, similarly, is told by a Rishi, or great sage, to Yudhisthira, at the close of day, during the banishment of the five Pandavas to the forest.

On this plan, more than half the countryside tales of Northern India could be woven into the Mahabharata when it was first thrown into form by some unknown hand, three or four centuries before Christ. It underwent its final recension not more than two or three hundred years later—a possible fifteen hundred years after the occurrence of the events which are its central theme. It is easy to see that this saga fulfils thus all the conditions of great epic poetry. The stories that it tells have been worked over by the imagination of singers and people for hundreds of years. They have become simple, direct, inevitable. They are spoken out of the inmost heart of a nation not yet dreaming of self-consciousness. They are nothing if not absolutely sincere.

Comparing the Mahabharata with the Iliad and Odyssey, we find it less formed, less highly-wrought; more amorphous, but also more brilliant and intense. To quote a great writer on Indian thought: "Outline is entirely lost in colour."

These characteristics do not hold good to the same extent of the second Indian epic, the Ramayana which has a closely-worked motive running throughout. This poem—the tale of the Exile of Sita and Rama—received its present form not long after the Mahabharata, early in the Buddhist period. It is supposed that under Buddhist influence the monastic life had come to be so honoured that the flower of the nation were drawn to it, rather than to the mingled responsibilities and joys of the home. The romantic reaction in ideals which was inevitable gathered itself about the ancient theme of a princely couple of the house of Oudh, in whom all that was precious in monasticism was found blended with all that was desirable in sovereignty and love. The strong and quiet story spoke straight to the heart of the people, and **to this day there are no characters so beloved by the masses as those of the Ramayana, no one force that goes so far towards the moulding of Indian womanhood, as the ever-living touch of the little hand of that Sita who is held to have been Queen of Ayodhya thousands of years ago.**

The Ramayana, then, is a love-story which grew up and came to its flowering in the beginning of the Christian era. But it is unlike all other romances of that early epoch in the subtlety and distinctiveness of its various characters, and in the complexity of its interpretation of life. For though humanity itself may differ little from age to age, we have been accustomed to look for a definite growth in its literary self—reflection. We expect primitive poetry to be preoccupied with events, portraying men and women only in bold outline, as they move with simple grandeur through their fate. We do not look to it for subtle analysis of motive, or any exact mingling of the sweet and bitter cup of the personal life.

The progress of literature up to this time has been largely, as we think, the intensifying recognition Of human variation within a given psychological area. And in making such a statement we take pains to eliminate from the word "progress" all sense of improvement, since Homer remains for ever superior to Browning.

Simply, we find in art a parallel to the physical process by which the race moves on from strong family and communal types to a universal individual divergence. An overwhelming appreciation of spiritual content is what we have been ready in Europe to call "the modern spirit". It is a question whether the name can stand, however, when the Indian Epics become better known; for, strangely enough, in spite of their age and the heroic nature of their matter, they are permeated with this very quality. **In the Ramayana especially, as incident leads to incident, we have to realise that this is no story told for our amusement; but a woman's soul laid bare before us, as she climbs from step to step of renunciation.**

Perhaps only those who are in touch with national aspiration can fully understand the roundness and plasticity of its drama, but even the most cursory reader must be struck with this insight and delicacy of the Ramayana.

It is more today than a completed work of art; it is still a means for the development of the popular imagination. Even amongst the written versions we find no two quite alike. All children are brought up on the story, yet those who can read the original Sanskrit are few in number. To meet this fact translations have been made into various vernaculars by great poets from time to time—into Bengali, for instance, by Krittibas, and into Hindi by Tulsidas. Special incidents again have been selected and worked up into great episodes in Sanskrit, by one and another, such as Bhavabhuti in his "Exile of Sita", or Datta in the "Epic of Ravana".

In these versions the story becomes more and more clearly defined. Pulsing through every Ramayana runs the Hindu reverence for Rama as man, husband, and king. This reverence may seek new modes of expression, but it can never admit that that which is expressed was at any time less than the ideal. Yet we must remember that **that ideal is, in the ancient terms, Oriental rather than Occidental. It belonged to a conception of duty that placed society far above the individual, and made the perfect king seek the good of his people without any consideraton for his own or his wife's happiness.** The fact that made his marriage perfect was its complete demonstration that it was as possible for two as for one to devote themselves first to the general weal. For the acquiescence of Sita is given in her long years of silent banishment. Once during that time, says one of the regional poets, she saw her husband as he passed through the forest where she was and kept silence still. And though the incident is an addition not found in the original it only serves to bring out more clearly the intention of the first poem, where every dumb moment of those twenty years speaks louder than words the wife's acquiescence in her husband's will.

Behind the vernacular translators stand all those old nurses and granddames on whose laps the poets themselves first heard the great tale; and it is their perfect freedom to give their own versions of each episode—as must any of us in recounting actual happenings—that keeps it fresh and living and explains its changes of tint in the hands of genius.

In the Mahabharata mighty warriors follow beautiful women, and great saints move to and fro across the scenes in a glittering melle. The local colour is rich to a fault. The poem abownds in descriptions of social customs, domestic comfort, the fashions of old armour and similar details. But it is in the conception of character which it reveals that is becomes most significant. Bhishma, the Indian Arthur, is there, with his perfect knighthood and awful purity of soul. Lancelot is there—a glorified Lancelot, whose only fall was the utterance of a half-truth once, with purpose to mislead—in the person of the young king, Yudhisthira. And Krishna, the Indian Christ, is there, in that guise of prince and leader of men that has given him the name in India of "The Perfect Incarnation". One of the rival houses consists of a family of no less than a hundred children, so that the multiplicity of persons and incidents is best left to the imagination. Yet certain main features belong to the treatment of all characters alike. For the attention of the poet-chronicler is fixed on the invisible shackles of selfhood that bind us all. He seems to be describing great events; in reality he does not for one instant forget that he is occupied with the history of souls, depicting the incidence of their experience and knowledge on the external world.

It is strange to us that as long as Bhishma remains a militant figure in the battle of Kurukshetra he is acting as generalissimo for what he regards as the worse cause of the two. He has done his best to prevent the war, but when it is determined on, he sets himself to obey his sovereign, in the place that is his own. He is filled, as the Indian poet represents him, with supernatural assurance that his side must lose, yet he strikes not a single blow either more or less for this consideration. In like manner it is told of Krishna that after he has done his utmost for peace in the interests of justice, he is approached by both parties for his aid, and that such is the calmness of his outlook on life that he submits the matter to a moral test. To one claimant he will give his armies; the other he will serve in person unarmed, he says, leaving the choice to themselves. It is clear that the man whose greed and ambition are plunging whole nations into war will not have the spiritual insight to choose the Divine Person for his champion, rather than great hosts. And he does not.

Such stories illustrate the Hindu endeavour to understand every man's relation to a given situation, and to read in conflicting lines of conduct that same irresistible necessity which, acting from within, hurls each one of us upon his fate. In this endeavour lies the real secret of that tolerance which has so puzzled observers in the Indian people. **Not only has there never been religious persecution among Hindus, but the sceptic, the atheist, or the Christian missionary is as free to preach on the steps of the temple as the believing priest.** The European correlative of the trait is found in the dramatist or novelist of genius who can represent the motives of opposing sides so as to draw equally upon our sympathy; but this has always been an exceptional ability with us, and not a common attitude of mind.

In the Mahabharata itself the most perfect expression of such reconciliation of opposites is perhaps found in the story of Shishupal, the enemy of Krishna. Shishupal's mother had won Krishna's promise that her son might sin against him a hundred times, and yet be forgiven. But this cup of error was already full, when his crowning blasphemy occurred.

Then, as all waited in suspense, from behind the Blessed Knight flashed forth the bright discus of Vishnu, and striking the helmet of Shishupal clove him through, even to the ground. And lo, before their eyes, the soul of that sinful one came forth like a mass of flame, and passed over and melted into the feet of Krishna. "For even the enemies of God go to salvation," says the old chronicler, "by thinking much upon Him."

Few characters in literature can rank with the heroic figure of young Karna. Dark with anger, but perfect in chivalry, he resents to the death a slight levelled at his birth, yet turns in the midst of princely acclaims to salute reverently the aged charioteer supposed to be his father. Full of a palpitating humanity is Draupadi, the Pandava Queen.

The end of Bhishma is like that of some ancient Norseman. Lying on the field of battle where he fell, he refuses to be moved, and asks only for a bed and pillow such as are fit for knightly bowmen. One of the young chiefs divines his meaning, and, stepping forward, shoots arrows into the earth till what was desired has been provided. And on his bed of arrows Bhishma dies.

Such are some of the characters who form the ideal world of the Hindu home. Absorbed in her "worship of the Feet of the Lord," the little girl sits for hours in her corner, praying, "Make me a wife like Sita! Give me a husband like Rama!" Each act or speech of the untrained boy rushing in from school, may remind some one, half-laughing, half-admiring, of Yudhisthira or Lakshman, of Rama or Arjuna, and the name is sure to be recalled. It is expected that each member of the family shall have his favourite hero, who will be to him a sort of patron saint, and may appear as the centre of the story, if he is bidden to recount it. Thus, when one tells the Ramayana, Ravana is the hero; another makes it Hanuman; only the books keep it always Sita and Rama. And it is well understood that the chosen ideal exercises a preponderant influence over one's own development. None could love Lakshman without growing more full of gentle courtesy and tender consideration for the needs of others; he who cares for Hanuman cannot fail to become more capable of supreme devotion and ready service. And justice itself must reign in the heart that adores Yudhisthira.

Journeying in the mountains at nightfall, one came upon the small open hut of the graindealer, and saw, round a tiny lamp, a boy reading the Ramayana in the vernacular to a circle of his elders. At the end of each stanza they bowed their heads to the earth, with the chant, "To dear Sita's bridegroom, great Rama, all hail!" The shopkeeper in the city counts out his wares to the customer, saying, "One (Ram), two (Ram), three (Ram)," and so on, relapsing into a dream of worship when the measuring is done. Nay, once at least it is told how at the "Four (Ram)" the blessed name was enough to touch the inmost soul of him who uttered it, and he rose up then and there and left the world behind him. The woman terrified at thunder calls on "Sita Ram!" and the bearers of the dead keep time to the cry of "Rama Nama Satya hai!" ("The name of the Lord alone is real!")

What philosophy by itself could never have done for the humble, what the laws of Manu have done only in some small measure for the few, that the Epics have done through unnumbered ages and are doing still for all classes alike. They are the perpetual Hinduisers, for they are the ideal embodiments of that form of life, that conception of conduct, of which laws and theories can give but the briefest abstract, yet towards which the hope and effort of every Hindu child must be directed.

We are in the habit of talking of the changeless East; and, though there is a certain truth in the phrase, there is also a large element of fallacy. **One of the most striking features of Hindu society during the past fifty years has been the readiness of the people to adopt a foreign form of culture and to compete with those who are native to that culture on equal terms. In medicine, in letters, in science, even in industry, where there has been opportunity, we are astonished at the intellectual adaptability of the race.** Is the mere beckoning of he finger of the nineteenth century enough to subvert predilections as old as Babylon and Nineveh? we ask, amazed. By no means.

Such changes as these are merely surface deep. The hauteur of the East lies in the very knowledge that its civilisation has nothing to fear from the social and intellectual experiments of its youngsters, or even from such complete changes of mental raiment as amongst newer peoples would constitute revolutions of thought, for the effort of Eastern civilisation has always been to the solitary end of moralising the individual, and in this way it differs essentially from Western systems of culture, which have striven rather for the most efficient use of materials. **If Alexander, capable of organising the largest number of his fellows most effectually for a combination of military, commercial, and scientific ends in that most difficult form, an armed expedition over hostile territory—if Alexander be taken as the type of Occidental genius, then, as the culminating example of the Oriental, we must name Buddha; for clear and intense conceptions of perfect renunciation and inner illumination are the hidden springs of Hindu living, around which the home itself is built.** These it is of which the Epics are the popular vehicles, these it is which give its persistence to Indian civilisation through the centuries, and this is why no examination syllabus, no alien's kindly inspiration, no foreigner's appreciation or contempt, can ever hope to have one iota of permanent influence on the national education at its core.

Reforming sects are very apt to reject what is much

cultivated amongst the Orthodox—the folklore that has grown up round the Epics in the Puranas and other literature. But to the poems themselves all cling fast. None fail to realise that they bear the mark of supreme literature, and so they remain a constant element, capable, like all great interpretations of life, of infinitely varied application, a treasure greater, because more greatly used than any Anger of Achilles, or Descent into Purgatory, amongst them all.

•••

15

HINDU WOMAN AS MOTHER

These eighteen centuries has Europe been dreaming of the idyll of the Oriental woman. For Asia is one, and the wondrous Maiden of all Christian art, form the Byzantines down to yesterday—who is she, of what is she aware, save that she is a simple Eastern mother? Of what fasts and vigils are we told in her case, that she should have known herself, or been known, as Queen of Saints? A rapt humility, as of one whose robe was always, indeed, her veil; a touch of deep silence, and that gracious richness of maternity which we can infer from the full and rounded sweetness of the Child who grew within her shadow—what more do we know of the Blessed Virgin than these things?

What more we may desire to know we can learn in the East itself-in India as well as anywhere. For in the period before Islam had defined itself, overflowing Chaldea, with the impulse, perhaps, of the pastoral life, become aggressive, to re-make the desert—in the days when Palestine and Lebanon were cultivated lands, inhabited by peasants of the early type, not as yet made a burnt-offering on the altar of crusading fury, in the closing centuries of the pre-Christian era—the common life of Syria had a still wider identity with that of Hindus than it has today. The ceremonial washings of Pharisees and Sadducees, the constant purifying of the cup and platter, the habitual repetition of a single name or prayer, which some later phase of the Christianising consciousness has stigmatised as "vain"—these things were not like, they were, what we know today as Hinduism, being merely those threads of the one great web of Asiatic life that happened to touch the Mediterranean coast.

And in matters so fundamental as the relation of mother and child, religious teachers come only to enforce the message of the race. Is it not said by the Prophet himself that the man who kisses the feet of his mother finds himself in Paradise?

Yet how frail and slight and young is often the mother so tenderly adored! No Madonna of the Sistine Chapel can give that lofty purity of brow or delicate untouched virginity of look of anyone of these Hindu mother-maidens, whose veil half covers, half reveals, as she rests on her left arm, her son!

The picture is too central to Indian life to have demanded literary idealising. Poetic and mythological presentments of the perfect wife there are in plenty: of motherhood, none. Only God is worshipped as such by men and children and by mothers themselves as the Holy Child! Here the half pathos of Western maternity, with its perpetual suggestion of the brood-hen whose fledglings are about to escape her, is gone, and an overwhelming sense of tenderness and union takes its place. To one's mother one always remains a baby. It would be unmanly to disguise the fact. And yet for her sake most of all it is needful to play the man, that she may have a support on which to lean in the hour of darkness and need. Even a wife has no power to bring division between a mother and her son, for the wife belongs almost more to her husband's mother than to himself. There can, therefore, be no jealousy at the entry of another woman into his life. Instead of this, it is she who urges the marriage; every offering is sent out in her name; and the procession that wends from the bridegroom's house to the bride's some few days before the wedding, bearing unguents and fragrant oils for the ceremonial bath, carries her loving invitation and goodwill to the new and longed for daughter.

Even in Indian home life, then, full as this is of intensity of sweetness, there is no other tie to be compared in depth to that which binds together the mother and her child. With the coming of her firstborn, be it boy or girl, the young wife has been advanced, as it were, out of the novitiate. She has become a member of the authoritative circle. It is as if the whole world recognises that henceforth there will be one soul at least to whom her every act is holy, before whom she is entirely without fault, and enters into the conspiracy of maintaining her child's reverence.

For there are no circumstances sufficient in Eastern eyes to justify criticism of a mother by her child. Their horror of the fault of Gertrude is almost exaggerated, yet Hamlet's spell is invariably broken when he speaks of the fact. To him, her sin should be sacred, beyond reproach; he ought not to be able to think of it as other than his own.

The freedom and pleasantries of filial sentiment in the West are thus largely wanting in that of the East. A determined stampede of babies of from three to six may, indeed, take place day after day through the room where their mother is at prayer. There may even be an attempt at such an hour to take the city by assault, the children leaping vociferously on the back of that good mother, whose quiet of conscience depends, as they well know, on her perfect silence, so that she can punish them only by turning towards them the sweetest of smiles. "Why, mother," said her family priest to one who appealed to him regarding devotions interrupted thus, "the Lord knows that you are a mother, and He makes allowance for these things!" But though, in the Oriental home, the wickedness of five years old may find such vent as this, the off-hand camaraderie that learns later to dub its parents" mater" and" governor" suggests a state little short of savagery, and the daughter who permits herself to precede her father is held guilty of sacrilege. The tenderness of parents corresponds to this veneration of children, and we only learn the secret of feelings so deep-rooted when we find that every child is a nurseling for its first two years of life. Consciousness and even thought are thus awakened long before the closest intimacy is broken, and a dependence that to us of the West is but a vague imagination, to the Eastern man or woman is a living memory.

How completely this may become an ingrained motive we see in the case of that Mogul Emperor who is remembered simply as "the Great". For Akbar had a foster-brother in the Rajput household whither his father Humayun had fled before his birth and where his first six years of life were passed, Akbar's mother dying, the Rajput Queen took the babe to nurse with her own son, and brought up the boys in this respect as brothers, though the guest was a Mussulman of Tamerlane's descent, and her own the proudest Hindu blood on earth. Events swept the children apart in boyhood, and, destiny fulfilling itself, he who came of a race of conquerors ascended the throne of Delhi, after many years, as Emperor of India. Then he found his Rajput subjects difficult indeed to subjugate. In them, the national idea renewed itself again and again, and insurrection followed insurrection. There was one name, morever, in every list of rebels, and men wondered at the indulgence with which the august ruler passed it by so often. At last some one ventured to point it out, protesting that justice must surely be done now. "Justice, my friend!" said the lofty Akbar, turning on his counsellor, "there is an ocean of milk between him and me, and that justice cannot cross!"

This long babyhood creates a tie that nothing can break. The thoughts and feelings of womanhood never become ridiculous in the eyes of the Indian man. It is no shame to him that his mother could not bear a separation; it is right and natural that he should be guided by this wish of hers. None but the hopelessly degraded ever reacts against woman's weakness in active cruelty. If one asks some hard worker in his old age to what he owes his habit of industry or his determined perseverance over detail, it is more than likely that his reply will take us back to his infancy and the wishes that a young mother, long dead, may have expressed for him. Or the man, in perplexity as to the course he should pursue, will go as naturally as a child, to test his question in the light of her feminine intuition. In all probability, she is utterly unlearned, but he knows well the directness of her mind, and judges rightly that wisdom lies in love and experience, having but little to do with letters.

Surely one of the sweetest happenings was that of a little boy of six who became in later life extremely distinguished. His mother, too shy to express the wish for instruction to her learned husband, confided in her son, and day after he would toddle home from the village school, slate and pencil in hand, to go once more through his morning's lesson with her, and so, with mutual secrecy, she was taught to read by her own child! With almost all great men in India the love of their mothers has been a passion. It is told of a famous Bengali judge who died some twenty-five years ago—one whose judicial decisions were recorded and quoted, even by the Englishmen who heard them, as precedents in English law, it is told of this man, when on his death-bed, that his mother stumbled and hurt her foot on the threshold of his room one morning, as she came after bathing to visit him. Another moment, and, weak as he was, he had crept across the floor, and lay before her, kissing the wounded foot again and again, and bathing it in hot tears of self-reproach for the pain it suffered. Such stories are remembered and repeated in Indian society, not because they occasion surprise, but because they make the man's own name holy. The death scene ,with Aase would redeem Peer Gynt himself. None who is sound in this basic relationship of life can be altogether corrupt in the rest, nor cun his decisions, however adverse, be completely repugnant to us. How curious are the disputes that agitate Christendom as to the sentiment one may fittingly indulge towards the mother. of a beloved Son! Is her supreme position in His life not self-evident? What, then, could be more convincing of union with Him than sweetness of feeling and words of endearment addressed to her? And so, with its wonderful simplicity, the great heart of the East sweeps aside our flimsy arguments and holds up to us the fact itself.

But it is not the great alone who worship motherhood in India. Never can I forget the long hours of one hot March day, when I sat by the bed-side of a boy who was dying of plague. His home was of the humblest, a mud hut with a thatched roof. His family were Shudras, or working-folk. Even his father, it appeared, could not read or write. The boy was eleven or twelve years of age, an only child, and he was doomed. The visitor's sole real usefulness lay in taking precautions against the spread of the disease.

Amongst the veiled and silent women who came and went at the other side of the little court where the boy lay, was one who slipped noiselessly to his bed-side whenever she could, and exposed herself to the infection with a recklessness born of ignorance. At last I attempted to reason with her, urging her, as gently as I could, to remain at some distance from the lad, and thus avoid the danger for herself and others.

She turned to obey without a word, but as she went the tears poured down her poor thin cheeks, and lifting the corner of her sari to wipe them away, she tried to stifle the sobs she could not altogether repress. At that moment the words reached me from the door-way. "She is his mother." What I did can be imagined. Suddenly I discovered that the boy must be fanned, and that there was a place behind his pillow out of the line of the air current. Here, with his head almost resting on her feet, his mother sat henceforth, crouched up, attending to her child through happy hours.

Often he would grow delirious, and forget her presence. Then he would toss his head from side to side, and his fever-lighted eyes stared blankly at me, while he uttered his one cry, "Ma! Ma! Mata ji!—Mother! Mother! honoured Mother!" To my Western ears it seemed a strange cry for a child of the slums! Sometimes, as memory returned, he would smile at me, mistaking me for her, and once he snatched at my hand and then carried his own to his lips. Sweet, unknown mother, forgive me these thefts of love, that rent the veil from a graciousness so perfect, an adoration so deep!

That day, alas, was their last together. All through the hours, the child had struggled to repeat the name of God. Late in the afternoon he stumbled on a hymn that was much sung at the time about tbe streets; but he could not say it, and it was my part to take up the words and stand repeating them beside him. A smile of relief passed over his face; he lay quiet for a moment. Then his breath came shorter and shorter, and as the sun set, with his mother's eyes upon his face, he died.

Of such stuff as this are the teeming millions of the Hindu people made. In moments of mortal agony, when Western lips would frame a prayer, perhaps half an oath, the groan that they utter is ever the cry of the child in its deepest need, "Oh, Mother!"

But it is easy to multiply instances. What we want is that epic of motherhood, of which each separate mother and her child are but a single line or stanza, that all-compelling imagination of the race, which must for ever be working itself out through the individual.

We talk glibly of Dante's "Vision of Hell". How many of us have looked into hell, or even seen it from afar off, that we should appreciate what it means to descend there? When the gloom of insanity falls upon the soul so that it turns to rend and destroy its dearest and best, when the blight of some dread imagination covers us with its shadow, is it lover, or child, or servant, who will still find in our maimed and maleficent presence his chiefest good? There is One indeed whom we cannot imagine as forsaking us. One whose will for us has been the law of righteousness, and yet for whose help we shall cry out instinctively in the moment of the commission of a crime. And like the love of God in this respect is, to Hindu thinking, that of a mother. Transcending the wife's, which may fluctuate with the sweetness bestowed upon it, the mother's affection, by its very nature, grows deeper with deep need, and follows the beloved even into hell. A yearning love that can never refuse us; a benediction that for ever abides with us; a presence from which we cannot grow away; a heart in which we are always safe; sweetness unfathomed, bond unbreakable, holiness without a shadow—all these indeed, and more, is motherhood. Small wonder that the innermost longing of every Hindu is to find himself at home in the Universe, with all that comes thereby of joy or sorrow, even as a baby lying against its mother's heart! This is the dream that is called Nirvana, Freedom. It is the ceasing from those preferences that withhold us that is called Renunciation.

The very word "mother" is held to be sacred, and good men offer it to good women for their protection. There is no timely service that may not be rendered to one, however young or beautiful, by the passing stranger, if only he first address her thus. Even a father, looking at some small daughter, and struggling to express the mystery of futurity that he beholds in her, may address her as "little mother". And the mother of the nation, Uma Haimavati, is portrayed always as a child, thought of always as a daughter of the house. In motherhood alone does marriage become holy; without it, the mere indulgence of affection has no right to be. This is the true secret of the longing for children. And to reach that height of worship in which the husband feels his wife to be his mother, is at once to crown and end all lower ties.

Who that has ever watched it can forget a Hindu woman's worship of the Holy Child? A small brass image of the Baby Krishna lies, or kneels at play, in a tiny cot, and through the hours of morning, after her bath and before her cooking, the woman, who may or may not herself be wife and mother, sits offering to this image flowers and the water of the bath, fruits, sweets, and other things—her oblations interspersed with constant acts of meditation and silent prayer. She is striving to worship God as the Child Saviour, struggling to think of herself as the Mother of God. She is ready enough to give her reason, if we ask her. "Does my feeling for my children change according to what they do for me?" she questions in return: "Even so should one love God. Mothers love most those who need most. Even so should one love God." The simple answer is worth a world of theology. Nor is it forgotten presently that the other children, made of flesh and blood, and answering to her call, are like-wise His images. In every moment of feeding, or training, or play, of serving or using or enjoying, she may make her dealing with these an act of devotion. It was her object, during the hours of worship, to come face to face with the Universal Self. Has she done this, or has she brooded over the ideal sentiment till she has made of herself the perfect mother?

By her child, again, her intention can never be doubted. She may turn on him now a smile and then a face of sorrow, now a word of praise and again an indignant reproach. But always, equally, she remains the mother. The heart of hearts of her deed is unfailing love. She knows well, too, that nothing her babies do can mean anything else. The sunny and the petulant, the obedient and the wilful, are only seeking so many different ways to express a selfsame dependence. To each she accords the welcome of his own nature. In such a reconciliation of opposites, in such a discovery of unity in variety, lies the whole effort and trend of Eastern religion.

For what thought is it that speaks supremely to India in the great word "Mother"? Is it not the vision of a love that never seeks to possess, that is, content simply to be—a giving that could not wish return: a radiance that we do not even dream of grasping, but in which we are content to bask, letting the eternal sunshine play around and through us?

And yet, and yet, was there ever an ideal of such strength as this, that was not firm-based on some form of discipline? **What, then, is the price that is paid by Hindu women for a worship so precious? The price is the absolute inviolability of marriage.** The worship is, at bottom, the worship of steadfastness and purity. If it were conceivable to the Hindu son that his mother could cease for one moment to be faithful to his father—whatever the provocation, the coldness, or even cruelty, to which she might be subjected-at that moment his idealism of her would become a living pain. **A widow remarried is no better in Hindu eyes than a woman of no character, and this is the case even where the marriage was only betrothal, and the young fiancee has become what we know as a child-widow.**

This inviolability of the marriage tie has nothing whatever to do with attraction and mutual love. Once a wife, always a wife, even though the bond be shared with others, or remain always only a name. That other men should be only as shadows to her, that her feet should be ready at all times to go forth on any path, even that of death, as the companion of her husband, these things constitute the purity of the wife in India. It is told of some wives with bated breath, how on hearing of the approaching death of the beloved, they have turned, smiling, and gone to sleep, saying, "I must precede, not follow!" and from that sleep they never woke again.

But if we probe deep enough, what, after all, is purity? Where and when can we say it is, and how are we to determine that here and now it is not? What is there sacred in one man's monopoly? Or if it be of the mind alone, how can any physical test be rightly imposed?

Purity in everyone of its forms is the central pursuit of Indian life. But even the passion of this search grows pale beside the remorseless truthfulness of Hindu logic. There is ultimately, admits India, no single thing called purity: there is the great life of the impersonal, surging through the individual, and each virtue in its turn is but another name for this.

And so the idea of the sanctity of motherhood, based on the inviolability of marriage, finds due and logical completion in the still greater doctrine of the sacredness of religious celibacy. It is the towering ideal of the supersocial life—Has the blazing sun to a fire-fly" compared to that of the householder—which gives sanction and relation to all social bonds. In proportion as the fact of manhood becomes priesthood, does it attain its full glory; and the mother, entering into the prison of a sweet dedication, that she may bestow upon her own child the mystery of breath, makes possible in his eyes, by the perfect stainlessness of her devotion, the thought of that other life whose head touches the stars.

•••

16

ONCE A WIFE, ALWAYS A WIFE

Of the ideal woman of the religious orders the West today has very little notion. Teresa and Catherine are now but high-sounding names in history; Beatrice, a true daughter of the Church, is beloved only of the poets; and Joan of Arc, better understood, is rightly felt to be by birth the nun, but by genius the knight. Yet without some deeper sense of kindred with these it will be hard to understand a Hindu marriage, for the **Indian bride comes to her husband much as the Western woman might enter a church.** Their love is a devotion, to be offered in secret. They know well that they are the strongest influence, each in the other's life, but before the family there can be no assertion of the fact. Their first duty is to see that the claims of others are duly met; for the ideal is that a wife shall, if that be possible, love her husband's people as she never loved her own; that the new parents shall be more to her than the old; that she can bring no gift into their home so fair," as a full and abundant daughterhood and a confirmation of their supreme place in their son's love. Both husband and wife must set their faces towards the welfare of the family. This, and not that they should love each other before all created beings, is the primal intention of marriage. Yet for the woman supreme love also is a duty. Only to the man his mother must stand always first. In some sense, therefore, the relation is not mutual. And this is in full accordance with the national sentiment, which stigmatises affection that asks for equal return as "shopkeeping". When her husband is present or before honoured guests, the young wife may not obtrude herself on the attention of her elders. She sits silent, with veil down, plying a fan or doing some little service for the new mother. But through the work of the day she is a trusted helpmeet, and the relation is often very sweet. Nothing is so easy to distinguish as the educational impress of the good mother-in-law. Dignity, with gaiety and freedom, is its great feature. The good breeding of the Hindu woman is so perfect that it is not noticed till one comes across the exception—some spoilt child, perhaps, who, as heiress or beauty has been too much indulged; and her self-assertiveness and want of restraint, though the same behaviour might seem decorous enough in an English girl of her age, will serve as some measure for the real value of the common standard.

It is not merely in her quietness and modesty, however, that the daughter-in-law betrays good training. She has what remains with her throughout life—a *savoir faire* that nothing can disturb. I have never known this broken; and I saw an extraordinary instance of it when a friend, the shyest of orthodox women, consented to have her photograph taken for one who begged it with urgency. She stipulated, naturally, that it should be done by a woman. But this was found to be impossible. "Then let it be an Englishman," she said with a sigh, evidently shrinking painfully from the idea of a man, yet feeling that the greater the race-distance the less would be the impropriety. The morning came, and the Englishman arrived, but in the Indian gentlewoman who faced him there was no trace of self-consciousness or fear. A superb indifference carried her through the ordeal, and would have been a sufficient protection in some real difficulty.

All the sons of a Hindu household bring their wives home to their mother's care, and she, having married her own daughters into other women's families, takes these in their place. There is thus a constant bubbling of young life about the elderly woman, and her own position becomes a mixture of the mother-suzeraine and lady abbess. She is well aware of the gossip and laughter of the girls amongst themselves, though they become so demure at her entrance. Whispering goes on in corners and merriment waxes high even in her presence, but she ignores it discreetly, and devotes her attention to persons of her own age. In the early summer mornings she smiles indulgently to find that one and another slipped away last night from-her proper sleeping-place and betook herself to the roof, half for the coolness and half for the mysterious joys of girls' midnight gossip.

The relationship, however, is as far from familiarity as that of any kind and trusted prioress with her novices.

The element of banter and freedom has another outlet, in the grandmother or whatever aged woman may take that place in the community house. Just as at home the little one had coaxed and appealed against the decisions of father or mother to the ever-ready granddame, so, now that she is a bride, she finds some old woman in her husband's home who has given up her cares into younger hands and is ready to forego all responsibility in the sweetness of becoming a confidante. One can imagine the rest. There must be many a difficulty, many a perplexity, in the new surroundings, but to them all old age can find some parallel. Looking back into her own memories, the grandmother tells of the questions that troubled her when she also was a bride, of the mistakes that she made, and the solutions that offered. Young and old take counsel together, and there is even the possibility that when a mother-in-law is unsympathetic, her own mother-in-law may intervene on behalf of a grandson's wife. Before the grandmother, therefore, there is none of that weight of reverence which can never be lightened in the mother's presence. Even the veil need not be dropped. The familiar "thou" takes the place of the stately "you" and there is no respect shown by frigid reserve.

Long ago, when a child's solemn betrothal often took place at seven or eight years of age, it was to gratify the old people's desire to have more children about them that the tiny maidens were brought into the house. It was on the grandmother's lap that the little ones were made acquainted; it was she and her husband who watched anxiously to see that they took to each other; it was they again who petted and comforted the minute grand-daughter-in-law in her hours of home-sickness. Marriage has grown later nowadays, in answer amongst other things to the pressure of an increasing poverty, and it does not happen so often that an old man is seen in the bazaar buying consoling gifts for the baby brides at home. But the same instinct still obtains, of making the new home a place of choice, when between her twelfth and fourteenth year—the girl's age at her first and second marriages—the young couple visit alternately in each other's families.

The Hindu theory is that a long vista of common memory adds sweetness even to the marriage tie, and whether we think this true or not, we have all known happy marriages on such a basis. But about the mutual sentiment of old and young there can be no theory, because there is no possibility of doubt. In all countries in the world it is recognised as amongst the happiest things in life. The reminiscence of Arjuna, one of the heroes of the great War-Epic, gives us the Indian explanation of this fact. "I climbed on his knee," he says, speaking of the aged knight Bhishma, head of his house, "all hot and dusty from my play, and flinging my arms about his neck, I called him 'Father'." "Nay, my child", he replied, as he held me to his breast, "not thy father but thy father's father!" With each generation, that is to say, the tie has deepened and intensified.

In all cases where one or two hundred persons live under the same roof, a complex etiquette grows up, by which gradations of rank and deference are rigidly defined. Under the Hindu system this fund of observation has so accumu-lated that it amounts now to an accomplished culture—a completed criticism of life—rich in quaint and delightful suggestions for humanity everywhere. We may not know why a mother's relatives are apt to be dearer than a father's, but the statement will be approved as soon as made. It has not occurred to us that our relations to an elder sister and a younger are not the same; in India there is a different word for each, for whole worlds of sweetness lie a world apart in one name and the other to the Hindu mind. Yet a cousin is constantly called brother or sister, the one relation being merged entirely in the other. The mere use of a language with this degree of definiteness implies an emotional training of extraordinary kind.

It is, of course, best suited to natures of great richness of feeling. In these, sentiment is developed in proportion to expression, and the same attitude that makes everyone in the village "Aunt" or "Uncle" to the children, produces an ultimate sense of kinship to the world. This is perhaps the commonest characteristic of Hindu men and women; shy at first, and passive to slight stimulus, as are all great forces, when once a relationship is established, they believe in it absolutely, blindly; are ready to go to the uttermost in its name; and forget entirely all distance of birth or difference of association. The weak point in the system appears when it has to deal with the harder, more arid class of natures. In these there is less inner response to the outer claim;

expressions of difference, therefore, become less sincere and more abject.

This is but a poor preparation for the open air of the modeen world, where seniority, sanctity, and rank have all to be more or less ignored, and man stands face to face with man, free and equal so far as the innate manhood of each can carry. But such persons—though, naturally enough, they cluster round the powerful foreigner as moths about a lamp—are the failures of Hinduism, not its types, and they are very few. In a perfected education, Western ideals of equality and struggle would present themselves to these for their choosing, while far away in Europe, maybe, hearts born too sensitive for their more rudimentary emotional surroundings would be thankful in turn to find life made richer by Indian conceptions of human relationship.

In a community like that of the Hindu home—as in all clan-systems—the characteristic virtue of every member must be a loyal recognition of common duties and dangers. And this is so. The wife who refused to share her husband's obligation to a widowed sister and her children was never known in India. Times of stress draw all parts of the vast group together; none of the blood can cry in vain for protection and support: even a "village-connection" (i.e., one who is kin by association only) finds refuge in his hour of need. This great nexus of responsibility takes the place of workhouse, hospital, orphanage, and the rest. Here the lucky and the unlucky are brought up side by side. *For to* the ripe and mellow genius of the East it has been always clear that the defenceless and unfortunate require a home, not a barrack.

Into this complex destiny the bride enters finally, about her fourteenth year. Till now she has been a happy child, running about in freedom, feet shod and head bare, eating and drinking what she would. Till now, life has been full of indulgences—for, her own parents, with the shadow of this early separation hanging over them, have seen no reason for a severity that must bring in its train an undying regret. From the moment of her betrothal, however, the girl's experience gradually changes. Just as the young nun, if she runs to find her thimble, will be sent back to bring it "more religiously", so about the newly married girl there grows a subtle atmosphere of recollectedness. The hair is parted, no longer childishly brushed back; and at the parting—showing just beyond the border of the veil with which her head now is always covered—appears a touch of vermilion, put there this morning as she dressed in token that she wished long life to her husband; much as one might, in taking up a fan, blow a kiss from its edge to some absent beloved one.

The young wife's feet are unshod, and the gold wedding bracelet on the left wrist, and a few ornaments appropriate to her new dignity, supply the only hint of girlish vanity. But she has more jewels. These that she wears daily are of plain gold, more or less richly worked, but on her wedding night she wore the Siti, or three-lined coronal, set with gems, and arms and neck were gay with flashing stones. All these were her dower, given by her father to be her personal property, and not even her husband can touch them without her consent, though he will add to them occasionally at festive moments. She will wear them all now and again, on great occasions but meanwhile the silver anklets and the golden necklet and a few bangles are enough for daily use. The girl knows her right to her own ornaments quite well, and the world will never hear how often the wife or the mother has hastened to give up the whole of this little resource in order that son or husband might weather a storm or receive an education. The one thing from which she will never part, however, unless widowhood lays its icy hand upon her life, is that ring of iron covered with gold and worn on the left wrist, which is the sign of the indissoluble bond of her marriage—her wedding-ring in fact.

With all the shyness of the religious novice comes the girl to her new home. Its very form, with its pillared courtyards, is that of a cloister. The constant dropping of the veil in the presence of a man, or before a senior, is the token of a real retirement, the sacrament of an actual seclusion, within which all the voices of the world lose distinctness and individuality, becoming but faint echoes of that which alone can call the soul and compel the eager feet. For India has no fear of too much worship. To her, all that exists is but a mighty curtain of appearances, trem-ulous now and again, with breaths from the unseen that it conceals. At any point, a pin-prick may pierce the great illusion, and the seeker become aware of the Infinite Reality beyond. And who so fitted to be the window of the Eternal Presence as that husband, who is at once most adored and loved of all created beings?

For there is a deep and general understanding of the fact that only in its own illumination, or its own feeling, can the soul find its highest individuation. To learn how she can offer most becomes thus the aim of the young wife's striving. All her dreams are of the saints-women mighty in renunciation: Sita, whose love found its richest expression in the life-long farewell that made her husband the ideal king; Sati, who died rather than hear a word against Shiva, even from her own father; and Uma, realising that her love was given in vain, yet pursuing the more eagerly the chosen path. "Be like Savitri," was her father's blessing, as he bade her the bridal farewell, and Savitri—the Alcestis of Indian story—was that maiden who followed even Death till she won back her husband's life.

Thus wifehood is thought great in proportion to its giving, not to its receiving. It would never occur to anyone, in writing fiction, or delineating actual character, to praise a woman's charms, as we praise Sarah Jennings', on the score that she retained her husband's affection during her whole life. **A good man, says the Hindu, does not fail his wife, but, apart from this, coquetry and vanity, however pleasing in their form, could never dignify marriage.** Lifelong intimacy, to be beautiful, must boast deeper foundations—the wife's love, daring all and asking for no return; the mother's gentleness that never changes; the friend's unswerving generosity. To the grave Oriental there is something indecorous in the discussion of the subject on any but this highest basis.

And yet Persia, the France of Asia, must have been a perpetual influence towards romanticism in Hindu life. There is said to be no love poetry in the world so impassioned as the Persian. The famous verse: Four eyes met. There were changes in two souls.

And now I cannot remember whether he is a man and I a woman,

Or he a woman and I a man. All I know is,

There were two: Love came, and there is one...

we must believe completely representative of its spirit. The Persian language, however, has only touched India through the Court of Delhi and through letters. It has been the possession of the Indo-Mohammedan, and of any man here and there who took the time and trouble to master its literature; but the world of Hindu womanhood has remained probably as remote from it as though it belonged to another planet.

This is not true to the same extent of the romantic aspect of Christianity. The letters taught in English schools result very much in novel-reading, and an indigenous school of fiction has grown up, in the form of books and magazines, which is likely to modify popular ideas on this subject profoundly. Meanwhile, and for long to come, it remains true that according to Hindu notions, the eyes of the bride and bridegroom are to be directed towards the welfare of the family and not of themselves, as the basis of society: it is the great springs of helpfulness and service, rather than those of mutual love and romantic happiness that marriage is expected to unloose. Selfish wives and jealous husbands there must be, as among all peoples. But it is a fact, nevertheless, that here the absolute stainlessness of the wife is considered but preliminary to the further virtue demanded of her, the sustaining of the honour of her husband's house.

With this clue it becomes easy to understand even what the West considers to be the anomalies of Hindu custom—the laws regarding rare cases of polygamy and adoption. For it is legally provided that if a woman remain childless, her husband may after seven years, and with her permission, take a second wife, in the hope of gaining a son to succeed to his place. On the European basis of individualism, the permission would probably be impossible to obtain; but with the Eastern sense of family obligation, this has not always been so, and I have myself met the son of such a marriage whose story was of peculiar interest. The elder wife had insisted that the time was come for the alternative to be tried, and had herself chosen the speaker's mother as the most beautiful girl she could find, for the husband. The marriage once over, she made every effort to make it a success, and welcomed the new wife as a younger sister. Not only this, but when the son was born, such was her tenderness that he was twelve years old before he knew that she was not his mother. After her death, however, the younger wife became head of the house. Amongst the children to be fed, there were degrees of kindred, certain adopted orphans, two or three cousins, and himself. He was the eldest of all, and protested loudly that he came in last, and his cousins only second, for his mother's attentions. "Nay, my child," she answered, with a Hindu woman's sweetness and good sense, "if I desired to neglect thee, I could not do it. Is it not right, then, first to serve those who have no protection against me?"

The family life which such a story discloses is singularly noble, and it is not necessary to suppose that polygamy entailed such generosities oftener than we find monogamy do amongst ourselves. In any case, the same tide that brings in individualism has swept away this custom;. and whereas it never was common it is now practically obsolete, except for princes and great nobles, and even amongst these classes there are signs of a radical change of custom.

"Where women are honoured, there the gods are pleased: where they are dishonoured, religious acts became of no avail." "In whatever family the husband is contented with his wife, and the wife with her husband, in that house will good fortune assuredly abide." Few books offer such delights to their readers as that known as the "Laws of Manu". It is in no sense a collection of Acts of Parliament, for the one attitude throughout is that of the witness, and the hastiest perusal shows that it represents the growth of custom during ages, and is in no sense the work of a single hand. This is indeed its first and most striking beauty. As must be, of course, it often happens that the superstition of a habit is stated as gravely as its original intent, but rarely so as to obscure that first significance, or leave it difficult of restoration; and from cover to cover the book throbs with the passion for justice, and the appreciation of fine shades of courtesy and taste, clothed in calm and judicial form.

Especially of this type are those dicta on the rights of women, which are household words in Indian homes. We all know the reaction of the written word on life. Fact once formulated as scripture acquires new emphasis, a certain occult significance seems to attach to it, and the words, "it is written" become terrible enough to affright the devil himself. In this way **the fear of a feminine curse has become a superstition in India, and I have seen even a low class mob fall back at the command of a single woman who opposed them.** For is it not written in the book of the law that "the house which is cursed by a woman perishes utterly, as if destroyed by a sacrifii:e for the death of an enemy"?—strange and graphic old phrase, pregnant of woe!

It is evident then that the laws of Manu are rather the unconscious expression of the spirit of the people than a declaration of the ideals towards which they strive. And for this reason they would afford the most reliable foundation for a healthy criticism of Indian custom. The conception of domestic happiness which they reveal is very complete, and no one who has seen the light on an Indian woman's face when it turns to her husband—as I have seen it in all parts of the country—can doubt that that conception is often realised in life. For if the characteristic emotion of the wife may be described as passionate reverence, that of the Hindu husband is certainly a measureless protection. If we may presume to analyse things so sacred as the great mutual trusts of life, it would seem that tenderness is the ruling note of the man's relation. Turning as he does to the memory of his own mother for the ideal perfection, there is again something of motherhood in what he brings to his wife. As a child might do, she cooks for him, and serves him, sitting before him as he eats to fan away the flies. As a disciple might, she prostrates herself before him, touching his feet with her head before receiving his blessing. It is not equality. No. But who talks of a vulgar equality, asks the Hindu wife, when she may have instead the unspeakable blessedness of offering worship?

And on the man's side, how is this received? Entirely without personal vanity. The idea that adoration is the soul's opportunity has sunk deep into the life of the people. And the husband can recognise his wife's right to realise her highest through him without ever forgetting that it is her power to love, not his worthiness of love, that is being displayed. Indeed, is not life everywhere of one tint in this regard? Does anything stir our reverence like an affection that we feel beyond our merit?

It is often glibly said that this habit of being served spoils the Indian man and renders him careless of the comfort of others. I have never found this to be so. It is true that Indian men do not rise when a woman enters, and remain standing till she is seated. Nor do they hasten to open the door through which she is about to pass. But then it is not according to the etiquette of their country to do these things. With regard to the last point, indeed, their idea is that man should precede woman, maintaining the tradition of the path-breaker in the jungle; and one of the most touching incidents in the national epic of heroic love is Sita's request to go first along the forest paths, in order to sweep the thorns from her husband's path with the end of her veil. Needless to say, such a paradox is not permitted.

Thus, honour for the weaker is expressed in one way in England and quite otherwise in Hindustan, but the heart of conduct is the same in both countries. The courtesy of husbands to their wives is quite unfailing amongst Hindus. "Thou shalt not strike a woman, even with a flower," is the proverb. His wife's desire for companionship on a journey is the first claim on a man. And it is very touching to notice how, as years go on, he leans more and more to the habit of addressing her as "O thou, mother of our son!" and presenting her to newcomers as "my children's mother," thus reflecting upon her his worship of motherhood. In early manhood he trusts to her advice to moderate the folly of his own rasher inclinations; in old age he becomes, as everywhere in the world, more entirely the eldest of her bairns, and she more and more the real head and centre of the home. But always she reins as she was at the beginning, Lakshmi, her husband's Goddess of Fortune.

In those first days he ate from no hand but his mother's or hers; and one of her devotions was the fast, not broken till he had eaten and their talk was over, though her evening meal might in this way be delayed till long past midnight. Now, with the responsibilities of her household upon her, she feeds a whole multitude before she takes her own turn, and still the mutual pact of soul and soul has not been broken by the strife of "rights". These two have all these years been each other's refuge against the world. And not once have they felt so separated as to offer thanks, or speak, either of the other, by name, as if head and hand could be different individuals!

On that first bridal evening, the little bride was borne before her young husband, and they were told that the moment was auspicious for their first shy look. Then the old Vedic fire was called to witness their rites of union; the girl flung the garland of flowers about the neck of her bridegroom, in exquisite symbolism of the bond that was to hold them; and finally they took seven steps together, hand in hand, while the priest chanted appropriate texts for each stage of life. Such was their wedding. Since then, the rights of one have been the rights of the other; joys, griefs, and duties have been held in common. Till now, if the bride of that distant night be entirely fortunate, the prayer of her childhood is fulfilled to her in the end of her days, that prayer that said:

> From the arms of husband and sons,
> When the Ganges is full of water,
> May I pass to the feet of the Lord.

It has seemed to me in watching Hindu couples that they were singular in the frequent attainment of a perfect intimacy. To what is this due? Is it the early association, or the fact that courtship comes after marriage, not before? Or is it the intense discipline of absolute reserve in the presence of others? The people themselves, where their attention- is called to it, attribute the fact to child-marriage. I remember asking a friend of my own, a man of wealth and cultivation, orthodox and childless, "If you could put away personal considerations, and speak only from the outside, which do you think better in the abstract, our marriage-system or yours?"

He paused, and answered slowly, "I think—ours; for I cannot conceive that two people could grow into each other, as my wife and I have done, under any other."

Amongst the luxuries of the West I have sometimes thought that the deepening of the human tie was proportionate to simplicity of surroundings. A people to whom all complexity of externals is impossible must live by thought and feeling, or perish in the wilderness.

But whatever be the truth on this point, I have seen clearly and constantly that the master-note by which the Hindu woman's life can be undetstood in the West is that of the religious life. This is so, even with the wife. Cloistered and veiled, she devotes herself to one name, one thought, yet is never known to betray the fact, even as the nun steals away in secret to kneel before the Blessed Sacrament. The ideal that she, like the nun, pursues, is that of a vision which merges the finite in the infinite, making strong to mock at separation, or even at change. And the point to be reached in practice is that where the whole world is made beautiful by the presence in it of the beloved, where the hungry are fed, and the needy relieved, out of a joyful recognition that they wear a common humanity with his; and where, above all, the sense of unrest and dissatisfaction is gone for ever, in the overflowing fulness of a love that asks no return except the power of more abundant loving.

•••

17

MY ANALYSIS OF CASTE

A graver intellectual confusion than that caused by the non-translation of the word Caste[1] there has seldom been. The assumed impossibility of finding an equivalent for the idea in English has led to the belief that there is something mysterious and unprecedented in the institution. People become bewildered as to whether it is a religious or a social obligation. Everyone demands of the reformer a conflict with it. The whole question grows obscure and irritating.

Yet all this time we have had an exact synonym for the word, and the parallel is the closer since our word connotes the same debatable borderland between morals and good taste. Caste ought to stand translated as honour. With Oriental quaintness, it is true, India has given a certain rigidity to this idea, but her analysis of the thing itself is as profound as it is acute.

Our conduct is commonly governed far more by social habit than by considerations of right and wrong.

1. The word 'Caste' is of Portugese origin.

When the tide of the ethical struggle has once set in over some matter, we may regard ourselves, as already half-lost. Why are my friend's open letters absolutely safe in my presence, though I am longing for the information they convey? Why can money given for one purpose not be used for another, when all the canons of common sense and expediency urge that it should? Who will confess to an effort in speaking the truth at any cost whatever? Why, when I am annoyed, do I not express myself in the language of Billingsgate? To each of which questions one would reply, somewhat haughtily, that the point was one of honour, or, that such happened to be the custom of one's class.

Yet if we examine into the sanction which honour can invoke there is nothing beyond a rare exercise of the power of ostracism. **The Church excommuni-cates, the law imprisons, but society merely "cuts" the offender in the street, Yet which of these three inflicts the deepest wound? It is as true of London as of Banaras that caste law is the last and finest that controls a man.**

There is another point about our Western conception of noblesse oblige. Few as the persons may be who could formulate their sentiment, the fact pervades the whole of the social area. Each class has its own honour. If honourable employers feel compelled to think of the comfort of their workers, honourable servants feel equally compelled to keep their lips shut on their masters' affairs, and either responds to an appeal in the name of his ideal.

The weaknesses of caste everywhere are manifold. For society, like the individual, is always apt to insist upon the tithing of mint and rue, and to neglect the weightier matters of the law. But it is not usually the martyr who marks its worst failure. He is the white dove cast forth by crows, that is, a member of a higher tried by consensus of the lower castes. We have here a case of government usurping the functions of society, much as if the head master should exercise authority in a dispute among boys.

The question of the inner trend or intention of the social movement must form the law in whose name all doubtful cases are tried. And, while it is never easy to determine the point accurately for one's own people, in the case of the Hindu race the supreme purpose of their past evolution is quite apparent. **Even a cursory reading of the Laws of Manu displays Indian society as united in a great co-operation for the preservation of ancient race-treasure of Sanskrit literature.**

The feeling must have grown up when the Vedas alone required conserving, and the families entrusted with various portions were encouraged to become in all ways dependent on the community, that every energy might be devoted to the task in hand. This is the real meaning of prostration at the feet of Brahmins, of the great merit acquired by feeding them, and of the terror of the crime of killing one. It is not the man, it is race-culture that is destroyed by such an act.

As ages went on and the Upanishads and other things were added to the store, that which was hitherto memorised became entrusted to writing. The Vedas became scriptures—and now the method of psychology, of astronomy, of mathematics, made themselves felt as integral parts of the Aryan treasure, in common with Sanskrit literature. This widened the conception of culture without liberalising the social bearings of the question, and **the Brahmin caste continued to be recognised as the natural guardians of all learning,** the old religious compositions being still regarded as the type.

If we ask how it happened that the Aryan folk became so early conscious of their responsibility in the matter of Sanskrit letters, there can be only one answer. **They found themselves in the presence of other and unlearned races.** This point brings us to the question of the origin of strongly differentiated castes in general. In its nature caste is, as we have seen, honour; that is to say, an ideal sentiment by whose means society spontaneously protects itself from some danger against which it is otherwise defenceless. For instance, life in Texas having been for many years dependent on the possession of horses, and safeguards against the horse-thief being few and difficult, he came to be the object of unprecedented social abhorrence. Horse-stealing was the last crime a lost soul would stoop to. In a similar way, as some think, may have grown up the Indian feeling about cow-killing.

If the cattle, in time of stress, were killed for food, agriculture would be unable to take a new start, and so a people accustomed to eat beef grasped the situation perhaps, and renounced the practice. But since these two sentiments pervade whole nations, they are not exactly what we are accustomed to think of as caste, inasmuch as in the latter there is a distinct gradation of rank connected with the sentiment. Here we have an occupational group giving birth immediately to the ideal which is necessary to its safety. Throughout the worlds of love, of war, and of work, indeed, honour is an instinct the very greatest potency. How few men, after all, desert to an enemy as spies! How strong is the feeling of class-obligation amongst servants and working men! This element is very evident in the Indian industrial castes, which are often simply hereditary trade-unions. No Englishman is so powerful, nor is any Hindu so hungry, that one man could be bribed to take up the trade of another. Nothing would induce the dairyman, for instance, to take charge of a horse, or a laundryman to assist the household. *

But the very strongest, and perhaps also ugliest of all possible roots of caste is the sense of race, the caste of blood. We have an instance of this in the animosity that divides white men from negroes in the United States, and we have other instances, less talked of, all up and down our vast British possessions. There is probably no other emotion so inhuman which receives such universal sympathy as this. For it is fundamentally the physical instinct of a vigorous type to protect itself from fusion. And both sides participate in the revulsion. Here we have the secret of rigid caste, for the only rigid caste is hereditary, and of hereditary caste the essential characteristic is the refusal of intermarriage.

Granting, then, what could not well be denied, that the Aryan forefathers found themselves in India face to face with inferior and aboriginal races, what may we gather, from the nature of the caste system today, to have been the elements of the problem, as they more or less clearly perceived it?

Those elments we may infer to have been four in number:

1. They desired above all things to preserve the honour of their daughters from marriage with lower and savage peoples. Exclusion from marriage with any but one's own caste became the rigorous rule, the penalty fell on the father and the family that permitted a woman to go unguarded on this head. To this day, if a son marries beneath caste he degrades himself; but if a daughter be wrongly given, the whole family becomes outcasted.
2. They seem to have desired to preserve the aboriginal races, on the one hand from extermination, and on the other from slavery of the person—two solutions which seemed later the only alternatives to Aryan persons in a similar position!

Those aborigines, therefore, who became dependent on the Aryan population, had their definite place assigned them in the scale of labour, and their occupations were secured to them by the contempt of the superior race.

We must not forget, in the apparent harshness of this convention, its large factor of hygienic caution.

The aborigines were often carrion-eaters, and always uncleanly in comparison with their neighbours. It was natural enough, therefore, that there should be a refusal to drink the same water, and so on.

On the other hand, it is one of the mistakes of caste everywhere, that it institutionalises and perpetuates an inequality which might have been minimised. But we must not forget, in the case of the Indian system, the two greater evils which were avoided altogether.

3. The Aryans realised very clearly that it was not only their race but also their civilisation that must be maintained in its purity. The word Aryan implies one acquainted with the processes of agriculture, an *earer* of the ground, to use an Elizabethan word—accustomed, therefore, to a fixed and industrialised mode of living, evidently in contrast to others who were not.

Fire and the processes of cooking and eating food are easily distinguished as the core of the personal life and establishment in a climate where habits can at any time be made so simple as in India. It is these that can never be dispensed with, though they may be arranged for tonight in a palace, and tomorrow in the jungle under a tree.

In view, then, of the necessity of safeguarding the system of manners, grew up the restrictions against eating with those of lower caste, or allowing them to touch the food and wants of their betters. The fact that the Aryan could eat food cooked by Aryan hands alone, implied that the strictest preliminaries of bathing had been complied with.

By a continuous crystallisation, all caste laws—from being the enunciation of broad canons of refinement as between Aryan and non-Aryan—came to be the regular caste-barriers between one class and another of the same race. In this way they lost their invidious character.

It is undeniable that this caste of the kitchen so wittily named "don't touchism" by a modem Hindu leader, lends itself to abuse and becomes an instrument of petty persecution more readily than the inter-marriage laws. Some of the saddest instances of caste-failure have occurred here. Nevertheless, the original intention remains clear and true, and is by no means completely obscured, even with the lapse of ages.

4. It was, however, in their perception of the fourth element of the problem that the early Aryans triumphantly solved the riddle of Humanity. They seem to have seen clearly that amongst the aborigines of India themselves were many degrees of social development already existent, and that these must be preserved and encouraged to progress.

From such a comprehension of the situation sprang the long and still growing graduation of non-Aryan castes, some of which have established themselves in the course of ages within the Aryan pale. Marriage, for instance, is an elaborate and expensive social function in the highest classes. But as we descend it becomes easier, till amongst the Baghdis, Bauris, and other aboriginal castes, almost any connection is ratified by the recognition of women and children. This is a point in which the Eastern scores over Western development; for in Europe the Church has caused to be reckoned as immoral what might, with more philosophy, have been treated as the lingering customs of sub-organised race-strata.

As is the nature of caste, mere social prestige constitutes a perpetual stimulus and invitation to rise, which means in this case to increase the number of daily baths and the cleanliness of cooking, and to restrict to purer and finer kinds the materials used for food, approximating continually toward the Brahmin standard. For is it not true that *noblesse oblige*? This fact it is that makes Hinduism always the vigorous living banyan, driving civilisation deeper and wider as It grows, and not the fossilised antiquity superficial observers have supposed.

Such, then, is the historic picture of the rise of caste. The society thus originated fell into four main groups:

1. Priests and learned men—the Brahmins;
2. The royal and military caste;
3. Professional men and merchants—the middle-class or bourgeoisie, as we say in Europe; and
4. The working people, or Shudras, in all their divisions.

   (Of the second group only the Rajput branch remains now stable. For the military caste, finding itself leaderless under the Maurya dynasty, is said to have become literary, and is certainly now absorbed in the bourgeoisie.)

This functional grouping, however, is traversed in all directions nowadays by the lines of caste. In the mountains it is no uncommon thing to find the Brahmin acting as a labourer, impressed as a coolie, or working as a farmer, and in the cities he belongs largely to the professional ranks. Many of India's most learned and active sons, on the other hand, belong to the third and even fourth divisions.

Every new community means a new caste in India. Thus we have the Mohammedan, the Christian, and the modern reform castes—of all of which one peculiarity is non-belief in the caste principle!—as well as others. And who shall determine, for instance, to which of the four main grades Mohammedanism, with its inclusion of peasant, citizen, and prince, belongs?

The fact is, if a man's mode of life be acceptable to his own caste-fellows, the rest of Indian society has no quarrel with it. And this autonomy of castes it is which is the real essential for social flexibility and fundamental equality. We must accept the Gita as an authoritative pronouncement on Hindu society. And the Gita rings with the constantly reiterated implication that "he who attains to God is the true man," while it interprets all life and responsibility as a means to this end. Thus, "Better one's own duty, though imperfect, than the duty of another well discharged. Better death in one's own duty; the duty of another brings on danger." We have to remember, too, that the Gita is made up of the very best of the Vedas and Upanishads, and was specially written for the benefit of women and the working classes, who, as destitute of classical learning, had little chance of studying these great scriptures. Another witness to the fact that spirituality has always been regarded in India as the common human possession lies in the Hindu word for religion itself—Dharma, or the manness of man. This is very striking. The whole weight of the conception is shifted away from creed, much more from caste or race, to that which is universal and permanent in each and every human being. And, last of all, **we may remember that the greatest historical teachers of Hinduism—Rama, Krishna, and Buddha, besides many of the Upanishadic period—were men of the second, or military, caste.**

No, the Brahmin was never in any sense the privileged monopolist of religion: he was a common channel of religious lore, because his actual function was Sanskrit culture, and **Sanskrit happens to be the vehicle of the most perfect religious thought that the world ever produced,** but "realisation" itself has always been recognised as a very different matter from this and, Brahmin or non-Brahmin, has been accepted wherever it appeared. The advantage that the priestly caste did undoubtedly enjoy, however, lay in the fact that in their case the etiquette of rank led directly to the highest inspiration, as the scholar's life, even in its routine, will be nearest to that of the saint.

One peculiarity of the place of the religious life in the Indian system is that it is an inclusive term for all forms of higher individuation. Theoretically, to the

Hindu mind, all genius is inspiration, the perception of unity; and the mathematics of Euclid or the sculpture of Michael Angelo would be as authentic an expression of the religious consciousness as the sainthood of Francis. **Only the result of this method of interpretation is that sainthood takes precedence of all others as the commonest form of greatness. Scientific research, as in the astronomy of Bhaskaracharya and the psychology of Patanjali, has not had sufficient opportunity of securing defined and independent scope. And literature has been yoked to the car of mythology as much as the art of medieaval Italy.**

Nevertheless, India is too well acquainted with genius to forget that the caste of the spirit is beyond human limitation, often beyond recognition. It is held that the best lower men can do for that brotherhood which asserts itself in the consciousness of greatness is to give it freedom. Hence a man can always be released from social obligations if he desire to live the life of ideas, of the soul.

This renunciation is Sannyasa, the Indian form of monasticism, and Sannyasa, theories to the contrary not withstanding, has always been open to all castes. Indeed, it is held that when the responsibilities of life are over, a man's duty is to leave the world and spend the remainder of his days in that state; and in some parts of Northern India one meets with "Tyagi Mehtars," or monastics who were by birth the lowest of the low.

Theoretically, the monk is caste-fellow of the whole

world, prepared to eat with any one; and where, by sheer dint of spirituality and self-discipline, such a feeling is realised, every Hindu in India considers the broken bread of this lover of mankind as sacramental food. It is usual, too, to eat from the hands of holy men without inquiry as to their standing when in the world.

One of the most interesting points in all this to a Western mind is the difference implied and established between the caste of priests or chaplains on the one hand, and the fact of spiritual realisation, outside all caste, on the other. Nothing in the Indian thought about life can be more striking than this.

The appearance of this new teacher, when he is powerful enough to be an important social phenomenon, is the historic origin of almost all new castes. The Sikh nation was formed in this way by a succession of Gurus. Chaitanya welcomed all castes to Vaishnavism and made it possible for them to rise thereby. The scavengers, too low to venture to claim either Hinduism or Mohammedanism as their own, were raised in consideration and self-respect by Guru Nanak and Lal Begi Mehtar—the last a saint of their own degree.

The preacher arises and proclaims the new idea. He gathers about him men of all classes: the educated, won to the service of his thought, the ignorant swept in by the radiance of his personality. Amongst his disciples, distinctions of caste break down. The whole group is stamped with his character: and prestige. Eventually, if it contain a preponderance of Brahmin elements, it may take rank with the best, carrying certain individuals up with it. But if it be composed chiefly of the scum of society, it will remain little considered; and yet, in the strength of its religious and intellectual significance may certainly claim to have progressed beyond its original point. Such is likely to be the fate of the present Christian converts.

Taking the history of Hinduism as a whole, we observe a great systole and diastole of caste, the Buddhist and the present Christian periods ranking as well-marked eras of fusion, while the intervening centuries are characterised by progressive definition, broken every now and then by a wave of reform which thought itself a movement towards caste abolition, but ended simply in the formation of a new group. For this is the fact in whicb all would-be reformations in India find at once their opportunity and their limit.

And it cannot be denied that **great benefits as well as great evils have accrued from caste. It is an institution that makes Hindu society the most eclectic with regard to ideas in the world. In India all religions have taken refuge**—the Parsi before the tide of Mussulman conquest; the Christians of Syria; the Jews. And they have received more than shelter—they have had the hospitality of a world that had nothing to fear from the foreigner who came in the name of freedom of conscience. **Caste made this possible, for in one sense it is the social formulation of defence minus all elements of aggression. Caste is race-continuity; it is the historic sense; it is the dignity of tradition and of purpose for the future. It**

is even more: it is the familiarity of a whole people in all its grades with the one supreme human motive—the notion of *noblesse oblige*. For though it is true that all men are influenced by this principle, it is all probably true that only the privileged are very conscious of the fact. Is caste, then, simply a burden, to be thrown off lightly, as a thing irksome and of little moment?

And yet, **if India is ever to regain national efficiency, this old device of the forefathers must be modified** in the process—exactly how, the indian people themselves can alone determine. **For India today has lost national efficiency.** This fact there is no gainsaying. Her needs now are not what they were yesterday.

Chief among all her needs is that of a passionate drawing together amongst her people themselves. The cry of home, of country, of place is yet to be heard by the soul of every Indian man and woman in Hindusthan, and following hard upon it must sound the overtones of labour and of race.

There are some who believe that there is no task beyond the ultimate power of the Hindu peoples to perform. The nation that has stood so persistently for righteousness through untold ages, has conserved such vast springs of vigour in itself, as must ultimately enable her to command Destiny.

●●●

Other Books on

PHILOSOPHY, RELIGION & CULTURE

1.	The Vital Truths of Hinduism (New)	250/-
2.	Philosophy India (New)	250/-
3.	The Dhammapada (New)	250/-
4.	The Last Days of Lord Buddha (New)	250/-
5.	Complete Book of Hindu Gods And Goddesses (New)	250/-
6.	Vatsyayana's Kamasutra Select and his Times	125/-
7.	The Kamasutra of Mallinaga Vatsyayana	125/-
8.	Judgment : No Aircrash No Death	250/-
9.	Patriot: Netaji Subhas Chandra Bose	250/-
10.	The Life of Lord Buddha	250/-
11.	The Discourses of Lord Buddha	250/-
12.	The Golden Book of Buddhism	250/-
13.	The Golden Book of Hinduism	250/-
14.	The Golden Book of Islam	250/-
15.	The Golden Book of Rigveda	250/-
16.	The Golden Book of Jainism	250/-
17.	The Golden Book of Upanishads	250/-
18.	Learn Rajayoga From Vivekananda	250/-
19.	Colossus Vivekananda Select	250/-
20.	Intellect India	250/-